Embracing My Sexuality and Emotions
SOUL

Embracing My Sexuality and Emotions
SOUL

By Ralph Ennis, Judy Gomoll, Rebecca Goldstone, Dennis Stokes, Christine Weddle

NAVPRESS

BE TRANSFORMED

BE TRANSFORMED

NavPress is the publishing ministry of The Navigators, an international Christian organization and leader in personal spiritual development. NavPress is committed to helping people grow spiritually and enjoy lives of meaning and hope through personal and group resources that are biblically rooted, culturally relevant, and highly practical.

For a free catalog go to www.NavPress.com
or call 1.800.366.7788 in the United States or 1.800.839.4769 in Canada.

Cover design by The DesignWorks Group, Jason Gabbert, www.thedesignworksgroup.com
Content Development Team: Ralph Ennis, Judy Gomoll, Rebecca Goldstone, Dennis Stokes, and
    Christine Weddle.

Consultation: Debbie Entsminger, Dr. Kimberly Knochel, Margo Balsis.
Thanks to the Navigator staff and students who field-tested this material.

Some of the anecdotal illustrations in this book are true to life and are included with the permission of the persons involved. All other illustrations are composites of real situations, and any resemblance to people living or dead is coincidental.

Printed in China

1 2 3 4 5 6 7 8 / 12 11 10 09 08

CONTENTS

BEFORE YOU SELECT THIS STUDY

. . . use caution in evaluating your group's readiness.

This study is not for everyone, no matter how interesting the topics may sound. And it is certainly not for every small group. The core topics in this study (sexuality, emotions, transforming change) are highly personal for everyone, and they are crucial — yet risky and painful for many — depending on one's background and past experiences.

Therefore, prepare carefully before launching into a group journey through this study. We recommend three prerequisites before your group considers going through this study together:

- Complete the study *IDENTITY: Becoming Who God Says I Am* together as a group first. This study lays the foundation of personal identity in Christ that one needs before exploring the narrower focus of sexuality and emotions.
- Discuss together the principles for small groups given on page 10. Make it your shared goal to grow in the qualities of a safe and healthy small group. Return to these guidelines occasionally to see how you're doing.
- Have at least three months of experience together as a small group before going through this study. This allows you to build trust and experience the journey of spiritual transformation together.

INTRODUCTION

This study continues the theme of identity from *IDENTITY: Becoming Who God Says I Am* — helping us discover God's perspective on who we really are (and are not) and learning to live authentically out of that true identity. If we want to find out what's true and good about us, we begin by discovering what's true and good about God and how He originally made us.

In the first five chapters you will explore the theme of sexuality, because your gender has been a core part of your God-given identity since you were born. Probably the first words spoken over you were "It's a boy!" or "It's a girl!" But learning to accept, enjoy, and even celebrate your gender is always a process. You will explore how to live life well as a sexual being, as well as learn what jealousy reveals about God's purposes for creating sexuality in the first place.

Another two chapters are devoted to exploring your emotional world, learning to listen to what our emotions are trying to tell us, and taking steps to experience God's healing touch in places of emotional pain.

The last two chapters invite you to explore the process of change and inner transformation that is at the heart of your spiritual journey by learning how to behold God. Ultimately we hope that these studies will release you to love yourself and live out of who God says you are as you experience God's redemption — so that you can better love God and others.

CHAPTER FLOW

Think of your time spent in each chapter as a mini journey — an exploratory trip into a significant topic on your way toward authentic spiritual transformation through Jesus.

Most chapters in each module have the following sections where you will "pause" your heart and mind along the way.

A SHORT STORY

Each is based on real life experiences.

PAUSE 1: EXPLORING WHAT GOD SAYS

This section encourages you to look at the Bible to see what God has said. We'll print out most of the verses for you, from a variety of Bible translations. But nothing beats reading your own Bible to make you comfortable in God's Word. You'll be reading the *New International Version* (NIV), unless stated otherwise. Sometimes we use *The Message* (MSG),

The New Living Translation (NLT), *The Living Bible* (TLB), or *The Amplified Bible* (AMP). As you move from chapter to chapter, you will gradually try different approaches to studying, processing, and applying these passages.

PAUSE 2: EXPLORING YOUR REALITY

Our information-driven society makes it easy to walk away from profound truth without considering what it really says about us. This section helps you identify where you are in terms of the topic, and how you got there. You will also explore what it might take for you to become more like Jesus.

PAUSE 3: COMING ALIVE TO GOD AND OTHERS

Our "What's-in-it-for-me?" culture often promotes self-centeredness and shallowness in our relationships. This section will help you examine biblical principles for knowing and relating to God and others with authenticity, honesty, humility, and love.

PAUSE 4: JOURNEYING FORWARD

Being connected with Jesus as your default lifestyle means learning to trust Him with what's true about you — all the way, every day. This section invites you to process and write out what you are learning as you live in Him, as well as what you're doing about what you are learning. We strongly encourage you to memorize the key verse provided for each chapter as a way of building this vital spiritual discipline into your journey.

DIGGING DEEPER

Like the photo album you make after a trip, in this optional section you can pause to recap and process the highlights of your experience so far. We'll give you a few "extras" if you want to explore and experience the topic of the chapter more deeply.

IMAGES

In each chapter we've included pictures and artwork to help you reflect on the topics. They are there to stimulate your imagination and heart when words fall short. Take time to gaze at the images and place yourself within these visual stories. If a photo disturbs you, that's okay; try to figure out why.

YOUR JOURNEY THROUGH EACH CHAPTER

For each chapter, expect to devote about an hour to personal preparation — more if you choose to do the optional "Digging Deeper" section. So pace yourself. You might try working a little at a time on a chapter — say, one section a day or twenty minutes a day or take a longer time of concentrated reflection. Find a rhythm that fits you best. Your group may want to consider discussing one chapter per session or dividing up the chapter and discussing it in two sessions.

FOR GROUP LEADERS

We've provided a leader's guide that can be downloaded at www.NavPress.com. Search for the ISBN or book title.

GETTING STARTED

To get the most from your study, we encourage you to do three simple things:

1. Read the verses meditatively, inviting the Holy Spirit to help you unpack what He wants you to understand from each verse. We've printed most passages from the *New International Version* (NIV) but occasionally quote from other translations for a fresh rendering. You may want to use your own Bible for any or all verses in this study.
2. Mark the verses to help you engage as you read. Be creative! Underline, draw circles or arrows ──▶, highlight, use colored pencils — whatever will help you process as you go.
3. Pray throughout your study, not just when you see a prayer-oriented question. Ask the Lord to shed light on what you're studying and to help you connect what you read to the realities in your life.

GUIDELINES FOR SMALL GROUPS

1. Confidentiality: Do not repeat anything said or heard inside the group to anyone outside the group. Refraining from gossip builds trust.
2. Safety: Respect each other's boundaries. Also accept each other's perceived realities without needing to comment or "fix" how someone feels or sees things at the moment. Nobody should feel forced to share anything that they prefer to keep private. Providing each other space and supportive care will promote safety.
3. "I" Statements: Be yourself; take off your masks. Share information only about yourself — not "we, they, or us."
4. Interference: Avoid giving advice, talking while someone else is sharing, or subtly competing by saying, "I'm just like you" or by sharing a similar story. Instead, listen attentively, learn from each other's life experiences, and offer brief and affirming feedback.
5. Individuality: Accept and enjoy the diversity in your group, including being at very different places on your spiritual journeys. Allow everyone (but don't force anyone) to discover areas of need or brokenness. Avoid probing or intrusive questioning, as well as tampering with or elaborating on each other's personal sharing.
6. Emotional Sharing: Expect and allow each other to experience a full range of emotion, even if this makes you uncomfortable. This might include crying, raising their voice, or being silent. When this happens, avoid interrupting, communicating that another's feelings are unacceptable or "bad." And don't touch or hug without

permission. Allow for times of quiet in your group because silence can be one of the most powerful healing environments.

7. Roadblocks and Obstacles: It is important to allow people to process their thoughts and feelings without needing to come to clear resolution. It is also normal to experience obstacles and setbacks. Remember that being stuck can be a catalyst for members to move forward. Trust the process!

8. Holy Spirit: Only God can perform the healing and growth needed in our hearts. The purpose of the group is to provide a place where the support, love, and acceptance of God can be modeled and felt and where the truth of God can be discovered and embraced.

9. Personal Responsibility: Recognize that true lifechange can occur only with God's help as we yield to His leading. The group can provide accountability through prayer and support.

10. Group Limits: Don't expect your group to provide therapy, counseling, or other in-depth one-to-one support for members. Know when to refer each other to someone outside your group who is better equipped to help.

BENEFITS OF HEALTHY GROUP PROCESS

1. A safe place to share vulnerably and honestly.
2. New relationships.
3. An opportunity to be listened to in an accepting and grace-filled environment.
4. A forum for embracing truth, gaining perspective, and growing spiritually at your own pace.

FOR GROUP DISCUSSION: After reading these guidelines together, discuss these questions in the group: Knowing myself, here are several practical things I will do to help make our group a safe place:

-
-
-

In a small group these specific things can make me feel unsafe:

-
-
-

Take time to pray together before you begin this journey.

CHAPTER 1
SEXUALITY: WHAT'S SACRED ABOUT IT?

Brittany is dating a pretty amazing guy, Chris, who is passionate about life and her. He has a heart for God as well. But lately they've been feeling the weight of what passion should look like in their relationship. Media images and their culture pressure them to do whatever feels good, and to express themselves through sex. But they also sincerely want to please God and value sex as something serious and deep — something that touches the soul.

When they're together, Brittany and Chris are both aware of the sexual tension between them. They want to really offer themselves to each other and genuinely care for each other. But it's still hard to know what the healthy way of expressing that is. What should be guarded and what should be shared?

Is your concept of sexuality limited to acts of sex? Or do you view sexuality as something much bigger — as a significant piece of your identity that makes you complete? In later chapters we'll explore biblical principles of <u>sexual behavior</u> — what we are to do with our sexuality. But in this chapter and the next one, let's consider the <u>meaning of sexuality</u> and how we are to <u>think and feel</u> about our sexuality. And what — if anything — our sexuality has to teach us about our God, who gifted us with sexuality as part of His image.

From all you know and have experienced up to this point in your life, how would you briefly describe "healthy sexuality"?

PAUSE 1_EXPLORING WHAT GOD SAYS

Today's world is looking for ways to integrate all of its fragmented parts. God made us spiritual beings. At the same time, He created us sexual beings (i.e., with gender and with sexual functions). There must be some link between our spirituality and our sexuality. We know the functions of sex: It's for reproduction and physical pleasure. But is that all? What's so good about sexuality? Is there anything sacred about it?

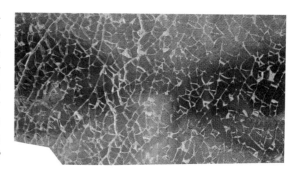

> Have you thought about sex as a metaphor for something larger — as a clue to the oneness God desires with you? Or do you see some sort of firewall between sexual intimacy and the worship of God?
>
> — PAULA RINEHART, *SEX AND THE SOUL OF A WOMAN*

Study these verses to discover what sexuality means — beyond physical pleasure. Fill the margins with your observations or questions about spirituality and sexuality — and the connections between them.

STORY 1: ADAM AND EVE (GENESIS 2)

SEXUALITY (BEING MALE OR FEMALE) IS ABOUT . . .

Not being alone in life.

GENESIS 2:18-25. The LORD God said, "It is <u>not good for the man to be alone</u>. I will make a helper suitable for him." . . . So the man gave names to all the livestock, the birds of the air and all the beasts of the field. But for Adam no suitable helper was found.

²¹So the LORD God caused the man to fall into a deep sleep; and while he was sleeping, he took one of the man's ribs and closed up the place with flesh. Then the LORD God made a woman from the rib he had taken out of the man, and he brought her to the man.

²³The man said, "This is now bone of my bones and flesh of my flesh; she shall be called 'woman,' for she was taken out of man." For this reason a

man will leave his father and mother and be united to his wife, and they will become one flesh.

25The man and his wife were both naked, and they felt no shame.

EPHESIANS 5:25-33. Husbands, love your wives, just as Christ loved the church and gave himself up for her to make her holy, cleansing her by the washing with water through the word, and to present her to himself as a radiant church, without stain or wrinkle or any other blemish, but holy and blameless. In this same way, husbands ought to love their wives as their own bodies. He who loves his wife loves himself. After all, no one ever hated his own body, but he feeds and cares for it, just as Christ does the church — for we are members of his body. "For this reason a man will leave his father and mother and be united to his wife, and the two will become one flesh." This is a profound mystery — but I am talking about Christ and the church. However, each one of you also must love his wife as he loves himself, and the wife must respect her husband.

In what ways is human sexuality also about the heart and spirit, not just the body?

Whether or not you are in an exclusive relationship now, how do you think love and respect impact the way you live out your sexuality?

Sexual intimacy binds people together physically, emotionally and spiritually. Each of these three elements is distinct from the others, yet they are dependent on one another at the same time. Sex is a beautiful mystery and a blessing when it is handled appropriately, and it is completely destructive when it is not.

— CRAIG GROSS AND MIKE FOSTER, *QUESTIONS YOU CAN'T ASK YOUR MAMA ABOUT SEX*

BACKGROUND:

We don't read very far in the Song of Songs before we realize two things: one, it contains exquisite love lyrics, and two, it is very explicit sexually. . . . Despite our sordid failures in love, we see here what we are created for, what God intends for us in the ecstasy and fulfillment that is celebrated in the lyricism of the Song. [Believers] read the Song on many levels: as the intimacy of marital love between man and woman, God's deep love for his people, Christ's Bridegroom love for His [Bride the] church, the [believer's] love for his or her Lord. It is a prism in which all the love of God in all the world, and all the responses of those who love and whom God loves, gathers and then separates into individual colors.

— Introduction to Song of
  Songs, *The Message*

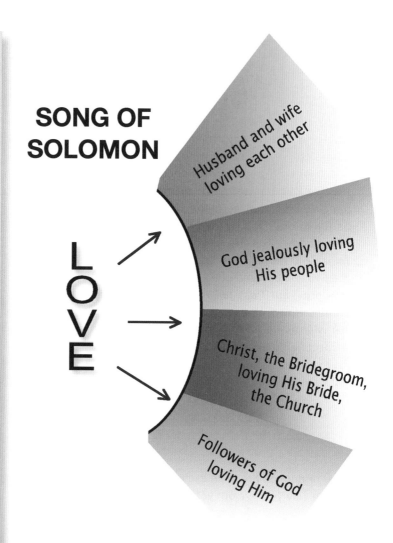

In the following verses from the most romantic book in the Bible, <u>mark anything you notice about the connections between sexuality and beauty, love, intimacy, or jealousy — or other themes.</u>

SEXUALITY IS ALSO ABOUT . . .

SONG OF SONGS 2:8-10.

Listen! My lover! Look! Here he comes,
   leaping across the mountains, bounding over the hills.
⁹My lover is like a gazelle or a young stag.
   Look! There he stands behind our wall, gazing
   through the windows, peering through the lattice.
¹⁰My lover spoke and said to me,
   "Arise, my darling, my beautiful one,
   and come with me."

SONG OF SONGS 7:10-13.

I belong to my lover, and his desire is for me.
¹¹Come, my lover, let us go to the countryside,
   let us spend the night in the villages.
¹²Let us go early to the vineyards to see if the vines have budded,
   if their blossoms have opened,
   and if the pomegranates are in bloom —
   there I will give you my love.
¹³The mandrakes send out their fragrance,
   and at our door is every delicacy, both new and old,
   that I have stored up for you, my lover.

SONG OF SONGS 8:4-7.

⁴Daughters of Jerusalem, I charge you:
   Do not arouse or awaken love until it so desires.
⁵Who is this coming up from the desert leaning on her lover?
   Under the apple tree I roused you;
   there your mother conceived you,
   there she who was in labor gave you birth.
⁶Place me like a seal over your heart, like a seal on your arm;
   for love is as strong as death,
   its jealousy unyielding as the grave.
   It burns like blazing fire, like a mighty flame.
⁷Many waters cannot quench love; rivers cannot wash it away.
   If one were to give all the wealth of his house for love,
   it would be utterly scorned.

Glance over your margin notes now and jot down any new insights about what sexuality is about — beyond its expression in physical pleasure.

PAUSE 2_EXPLORING YOUR REALITY

In a television interview, a rock star praised his wife for being his "soul mate." What do you think it means to be someone's soul mate?

How do you feel about finding a life partner who can be your soul mate?

What are some of our culture's messages on sex? How do they affect your view of yourself and/or others?

Modern man speaks of intercourse as "having sex." However, the Scriptures never speak this way. In biblical language, a man "knows" his wife. It is not an act; it is a relationship.

— PAUL BUBNA

◆ What is your response to the following statements?[1]

STATEMENT	POSITIVE / NEGATIVE? EXPLAIN
I am a sexual being.	
I am designed to express my womanhood / manhood in relationship.	
I am full of longing and desire.	
My sexuality is sacred.	

The Bible compares our relationship with God to the relationship between a bridegroom and his bride. As you read these verses, <u>write any observations about relating to God as newlyweds relate</u>.

> *ISAIAH 62:5. As a young man marries a maiden, so will your sons marry you; as a bridegroom rejoices over his bride, so will your God rejoice over you.*
>
> *2 CORINTHIANS 11:2. I [Paul] am jealous for you with a godly jealousy. I promised you to one husband, to Christ, so that I might present you as a pure virgin to him.*
>
> *REVELATION 19:7. Let us rejoice and be glad and give him glory! For the wedding of the Lamb has come, and his bride has made herself ready.*

One thing's for sure: newlyweds enjoy intimacy and oneness! That illustrates the connection between sexuality and spirituality. This oneness and intimacy found its origins in the Triune Godhead, where three unique personhoods make up one God. Our desire for sexual intimacy points to the greater reality: a deep longing for oneness with God.

— ANONYMOUS

Describe some aspects of a healthy relationship between a husband and wife.

---

[1] Questions marked with a ◆ are for personal reflection, not group discussion.

Now consider your relationship with Jesus from this viewpoint. How do you experience Him as your Bridegroom or Lover?

When Jesus prayed for His disciples at the Last Supper, He used the language of intimacy. Write your observations in the margin.

JOHN 17:21-24. I pray that they will all be one, just as you and I are one — as you are in me, Father, and I am in you. And may they be in us so that the world will believe you sent me.

²² I have given them the glory you gave me, so they may be one as we are one. I am in them and you are in me. May they experience such perfect unity that the world will know that you sent me and that you love them as much as you love me. Father, I want these whom you have given me to be with me where I am. Then they can see all the glory you gave me because you loved me even before the world began! (NLT)

PAU∫E 3_COMING ALIVE TO GOD AND OTHER∫

Bodies are central to the Christian story. Creation inaugurates bodies that are good, but the consequences of the fall are written on our bodies — our bodies will sweat as we labor in the fields, our bodies will hurt as we bear children, and, most centrally, our bodies will die. If the fall is written on the body, salvation happens in the body too. The kingdom of God is transmitted through Jesus's body and is sustained in Christ's Body, the church. Through the bodily suffering of Christ on the cross and the bodily resurrection of Christ from the dead, we are saved. Bodies are not just mirrors in which we see the consequence of the fall; they are also, in one theologian's phrase, "where God has chosen to find us in our fallenness." Bodies are who we are and where we live; they are not just things God created us with, but means of knowing Him and abiding with Him.

— LAUREN WINNER, *REAL SEX: THE NAKED TRUTH ABOUT CHASTITY*

∫TORY 3: ADAM AND EVE (GENE∫I∫ 3)

GENESIS 1:31 says that when God viewed His creation (including human sexuality) He declared it "very good." Then came the Fall, when Adam and Eve chose to rebel against God. In this rebellion of pride and envy, sin entered the world and contaminated everything — including the relationship between men and women. Before the Fall, it seems that Adam and Eve experienced:

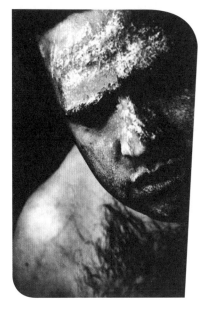

- gender clarity
- relational harmony
- sexual freedom within boundaries
- spiritual oneness with God and each other

So what happened to all that after the Fall? <u>What impact did that first sin have on all these parts of their lives?</u> Read the familiar story in Genesis 3:1-23. <u>Write your thoughts, questions, and conclusions.</u>

GENESIS 3:1-23

Imagine that we have bugged a conversation between Adam and Eve right after they were expelled from the garden. What do you suppose they might have said to one another?

What if Adam and Eve had understood that God was expressing His jealous love for them by setting one boundary — not trying to spoil their fun? If Adam and Eve had been jealous for God like God was jealous for them, how might that have influenced their choices?

God does not want to share your affections with any competitor. How does that affect you? How can it be for your best?

/TORY 4: THE CORINTHIAN BELIEVER/
(1 CORINTHIAN/ 6)

We still have more to learn about the sacredness of our sexuality. Paul explores this theme in his letter to the Corinthians. Remember that the culture of the ancient city of Corinth was a lot like ours. Sex saturated almost every side of life — even the religious side. When Paul started the first church there, a thousand priestesses and prostitutes entered the city every night as part of worship at the temple of Aphrodite, the goddess of love. Sexuality was so entwined with religion that the Corinthians were getting confused.

As you read the following passages, ask what they say about <u>how we should think about our sexuality — what sex is for and how to honor it</u>. Then summarize whatever you observe.

> *1 CORINTHIANS 6:12. You say, "I am allowed to do anything" — but not everything is good for you. And even though "I am allowed to do anything," I must not become a slave to anything. (NLT)*

TRUTH/ AND OB/ERVATION/:

I'm free to live fully as a sexual being. But not all sexual expression is good for me — in fact, some sexual habits can enslave me.

> *1 CORINTHIANS 6:13-14. You say, "Food was made for the stomach, and the stomach for food."(This is true, though someday God will do away with both of them.) But you can't say that our bodies were made for sexual immorality. They were made for the Lord, and the Lord cares about our bodies. And God will raise us from the dead by his power, just as he raised our Lord from the dead. (NLT)*

TRUTH/ AND OB/ERVATION/:

1 CORINTHIANS 6:15-17. Don't you realize that your bodies are actually parts of Christ? Should a man take his body, which is part of Christ, and join it to a prostitute? Never! And don't you realize that if a man joins himself to a prostitute, he becomes one body with her? For the Scriptures say, "The two are united into one." But the person who is joined to the Lord is one spirit with him. (NLT)

TRUTHS AND OBSERVATIONS:

1 CORINTHIANS 6:18-20. Run from sexual sin! No other sin so clearly affects the body as this one does. For sexual immorality is a sin against your own body. Don't you realize that your body is the temple of the Holy Spirit, who lives in you and was given to you by God? You do not belong to yourself, for God bought you with a high price. So you must honor God with your body. (NLT)

TRUTHS AND OBSERVATIONS:

From everything you've learned in your study so far, what do you think it means to be a sexually healthy single follower of Jesus in today's world?

How can healthy intimacy happen in friendships where discussing sexuality is okay, but it is protected as sacred?

Think about it: God could have given us the ability to reproduce without being male and female . . . earthworms do! What about God can we understand better because He created us as sexual beings?

PRAYER PAUSE

Stop for a moment to talk with Jesus about the ways you do or don't experience oneness and intimacy with Him. Perhaps invite Him to speak into that part of who you are, letting Him express His desire for you.

PAUSE 4_JOURNEYING FORWARD

ACTS 22:8,10.   Who are you, Lord?
What shall I do, Lord?

It's your life . . . it's your journey. So that means it's up to you how you respond to the ideas in this chapter. Pause 4 in every chapter will be like this one — completely open-ended to invite you to zero in on whatever specifically touched you most. Or whatever disturbed you the most. Whatever that is, grab on to it — don't gloss over it. During this final Pause, revisit that Scripture and respond to one or more of the reflective questions. Then pray about what step you should take to walk as Jesus did in the coming week.

At the end of every chapter we'll invite you to select one Bible verse or passage that you read, studied, listened to, or memorized during the week that was meaningful to you. Begin by copying the verse and its reference below so you'll be able to find it later.

We live in a world of images that deeply influence how we look at life. Choose a picture from this chapter that is meaningful or disturbing to you, and briefly explain why.

How have you experienced God this week?

Then, you'll be invited to select one or more of these reflective questions and journal your response. The point is not to answer all of the questions, but to help focus your reflection on what God is saying to you. Most chapters have a final Journal page to give you space to write.

Reflecting on what was most meaningful to you from this chapter, respond to one (or more) of these questions in the journal:

- Who are you, Lord? (an insight into God's character or heart)
- What shall I do, Lord? (an idea for practical application)
- Who shall I be, Lord? (a sense of personal identity)
- Other response?

JOURNAL

Think of the journal page as part of your spiritual fitness routine. Your spirit, heart, and mind have just finished some vigorous exercise. This is the cool-down phase. Not to be hurried. We suggest two things:

1. Journal on any of the preceding reflective questions.
2. Memorize and meditate on the Scripture memory verse below.

If at all possible, don't leave your study time without capturing in writing the most important things God revealed to you.

SUGGESTED MEMORY VERSE FOR THIS CHAPTER:

MEANING OF SEXUALITY — GENESIS 2:24-25

For this reason a man will leave his father and mother and be united to his wife, and they will become one flesh. The man and his wife were both naked, and they felt no shame.

Last, we'll suggest a key verse on the chapter's topic for you to memorize. If a different verse touched you more, feel free to substitute it. Taking 5–10 minutes right after completing the chapter study to memorize the verse may help anchor what you've learned in your heart and mind. After you have memorized the verse, check your accuracy. Try to write the verse from memory in the space below.

CHAPTER 2
SEXUALITY: WHAT'S JEALOUSY GOT TO DO WITH IT?

Twelve people in their twenties and thirties in a small group were asked this question: "Is jealousy a positive or a negative emotion to you?" All but one said it was negative. They turned to the woman who viewed jealousy as positive and asked why. She replied, "Because when my husband stopped being jealous for me, it was the end of our relationship."

What do you think the woman meant by "he stopped being jealous *for* me"?

God, in his mercy, longs to restore our souls. And the truth is that because He authored the mystery of sexuality, only He can restore our souls. Only God can touch the same deep places in you that are awakened in the experience of sex. He made you. The deep places of your soul belong to Him first. He gathers up the fragmented pieces of our shattered dreams — of our very selves — and knits them back together, and when He does it, it feels like a small Miracle.

— PAULA RINEHART, *SEX AND THE SOUL OF A WOMAN*

PAUSE 1_EXPLORING WHAT GOD SAYS

Like the members of that small group, most people view jealousy as a bad thing—a self-centered, suspicious, or bitter character flaw. There's only one problem with that. Exodus 34:14 says, "for the LORD, whose name is Jealous, is a jealous God." If the good Lord's name is Jealous, then jealousy can't be all bad, can it? In this chapter we'll explore how our sexuality and our spirituality reflect the godly jealousy that is part of being created in the image of our Jealous God.

And since everybody loves a love story, in this chapter you will get to read some of the Bible's romances. Be forewarned—some of them are more about lust than about love. Both kinds of stories have valuable and protective lessons for us.

STORY 1: SOLOMON AND HIS BRIDE
(SONG OF SOLOMON 8:4-7)

BACKGROUND

> Because Near Eastern peoples wore engraved signet rings on their fingers (Genesis 41:42, Jeremiah 22:24) or cylinder seals on neck cords (Genesis 38:18, Proverbs 3:3) to indicate identity or ownership (like a coat of arms or heraldic crest), the beloved in the Song of Songs asks her lover to place her as a seal on his arm (finger) and heart (Song of Songs 8:6). The woman's request for permanence in love thus implies both proximity (like the seal that is always present) and the action of being claimed (as her lover stamps his beloved like an official signature on his heart). Marital love is the strongest, most unyielding, and invincible force in human experience. As the grave will not give up the dead, so love will not surrender the loved one.
>
> — NIV Study Bible

From this passage, <u>what are some ways that good jealousy protects a relationship</u>?

SONG OF SOLOMON 8:4-7

Daughters of Jerusalem, I charge you:
    Do not arouse or awaken love until it so desires.
⁵ Who is this coming up from the desert leaning on her lover?
    Under the apple tree I roused you;
    there your mother conceived you,
    there she who was in labor gave you birth.

⁶ Place me like a seal over your heart,
  like a seal on your arm;
  for love is as strong as death,
  its jealousy unyielding as the grave.
  It burns like blazing fire,
  like a mighty flame.

⁷ Many waters cannot quench love;
  rivers cannot wash it away.
  If one were to give all the wealth of his house for love,
  it would be utterly scorned.

Would you want your spouse to be jealous for you — or not? Explain.

STORY 2: HOSEA AND GOMER (HOSEA 1–3)

We live in a world awash in love stories. Most of them are lies. They are not love stories at all — they are lust stories, sex-fantasy stories, domination stories. From the cradle we are fed on lies about love. . . . [The book of Hosea] is an astonishing story: a prophet commanded to marry a common whore and have children with her. It is an even more astonishing message: God loves us in just this way — goes after us at our worst, keeps after us until he gets us, and makes lovers of men and women who know nothing of real love.

— From the Introduction to Hosea, *The Message*

Begin by reading Hosea and Gomer's story in your Bible (Hosea chapters 1–3).

HISTORICAL BACKGROUND: The rest of the book of Hosea (chapters 4–14) describes the times Hosea and Gomer lived in. Israel was flagrantly violating the intimacy of the covenant relationship between them and God. They had turned to Baal worship, were sacrificing at pagan altars (including child sacrifices), worshipping a calf image, and were associating with sacred prostitutes at the sanctuaries. No wonder God accused them of "spiritual adultery." But alongside God's condemnation and judgment, this book proclaims God's compassion and jealous love that cannot let Israel go — no matter how much His heart breaks.

SCENE 1: HOSEA 1:1-11

Briefly summarize anything you observe about Hosea's love for Gomer and what this reveals about God's love for us.

SCENE 2: HOSEA 2:1-13

Briefly summarize anything you observe about Hosea's love for Gomer and what this reveals about God's love for us.

SCENE 3: HOSEA 2:14–3:5

Briefly summarize anything you observe about Hosea's love for Gomer and what this reveals about God's love for us.

Where do you think Gomer might have ended up if Hosea had not been jealous for her?

Do you think Gomer believed that she deserved Hosea's love? Why or why not?

Now try putting your discoveries together. God says that He loves us like Hosea loved Gomer. What does their story reveal about God's jealous love for us?

God created us as sexual beings. What does this say to you about God's heart?

PAUƧE 2_EXPLORING YOUR REALITY

Define or describe jealousy, as you understand it.

Envy is a close cousin emotionally to *jealousy.*
Envy means wanting to possess what rightfully belongs to someone else. When you say, "How did
you get tickets to the Super Bowl? I'm so jealous of you?" you are really feeling
envious, not jealous. Don't confuse envy with biblical jealousy. Describe a time you envied
somebody else for something they had that you wanted.

Pride can be either positive or negative, and so can jealousy. For example, Paul was proud of
the Corinthian believers (see 2 Corinthians 7:4 and 8:24). But God opposes the proud (James
4:6). Paul felt "godly jealousy" for the Corinthians to be devoted to Christ (2 Corinthians
11:2). But in the next chapter he warned them against "quarreling, jealousy, and outbursts of
anger" (2 Corinthians 12:20).

Consider these various descriptions of jealousy. Check the one that most closely matches
your concept of jealousy. Then check the one that you wish your lover would feel for you.

What Is Jealousy?

____ a. Feeling bitter and unhappy because of another's advantages, possessions, or luck
____ b. Feeling suspicious about the influence of a rival or competitor in a relationship
____ c. Demanding exclusive loyalty or adherence
____ d. Cherishing and vigilantly guarding what rightfully belongs to you; protectively watch-
         ful of a loved one
____ e. A protective, possessive, delighting, liberating cover for shame

Think of a time or situation (about you or someone you know) that fits this scenario (choose one):

- When you were jealous <u>for</u> someone else
- When someone should have been jealous <u>for</u> you, but wasn't

Not only is God jealous, but He has even taken Jealous as one of the names He wants to be known by.

> EXODUS 34:14. For the LORD, whose name is Jealous, is a jealous God.

Can you think of any time in the Bible when God acted out of jealous love for His people? Describe that time.

Godly jealousy is what burns in the heart of a person whose spouse is having an affair, or in the heart of a parent watching helplessly as a child is ensnared by addictions or destructive relationships. This is the positive face of jealousy that has been virtually lost in our culture.

— SEE THE *DIGGING DEEPER* SECTION

We all know that human sexuality is practiced in different forms: heterosexual, homosexual, and bisexual, for starters. People in all of these relationships feel the emotions of jealousy, envy, and shame. So consider this as one primary meaning of sexuality:

God has created us for relationship with each other and has also called us to Himself. Godly jealousy is a protective, possessive, delighting, and liberating covering that deals with the issue of shame in relationships.

The fact that we all feel jealousy reveals something about being created in God's image.

From what you have learned and experienced, complete these statements:

God is protective of us because . . .

God is possessive of us because . . .

God delights in us because . . .

God covers our shame because . . .

This is liberating because . . .

Consider any rivals for your wholehearted loyalty to God.
How does it make you feel to know that God is jealous by
being protectively watchful for you?

PAU∫E 3_COMING ALIVE TO GOD AND OTHER∫

Let's look at another Bible story to help us connect the dots about the meaning of sexuality and jealousy. It is a disturbing story about love, passion, marriage, betrayal, rejection, adultery, prostitution, and jealousy. Pay attention to what pieces of the story stir you personally. If it makes you aware of things in your own life or past, don't ignore them. Try to enter into what's being communicated.

∫TORY 3: GOD AND JERU∫ALEM (EZEHIEL 16)

Begin by reading the whole story (Ezekiel 16:1-42).

Notice that you can read this story from three angles: as a romantic tragedy about a man and his wife, as a historical allegory about God and the people of Israel, and as a modern parable about the Lord and us.

As you read this story, <u>write down your observations about love, sexuality, and jealousy.</u>

How might this story be different if the man had not been jealous for his wife?

Do you think the woman believed that she deserved his love? *Explain.*

In what sense have we all "prostituted" ourselves (been unfaithful) in our relationship with God?

How would humankind's story be different if God were not jealous for us?

How would your personal story be different if God hadn't been jealous for you?

Why do you think God chose such romantic and sexual imagery to depict the spiritual world?

What does this story in Ezekiel 16 add to your understanding about who God is and what He is like?

What does it reveal about why God created us with sexuality?

PRAYER PAUSE

Close in a time of prayer. Some options:

- Tell God how you have (or have not) experienced His jealous love for you, and how you feel about that.
- Express your desire to enjoy intimacy and oneness — with Him, with others.
- Also confess any fears you have about the whole area of intimacy — both sexual intimacy and soul intimacy.
- Ask Him to show you anything He wants you to change in order to honor your own sexuality (and others' sexuality) and to keep it sacred.

PAUSE 4_JOURNEYING FORWARD

ACTS 22:8,10.   Who are you, Lord?
                What shall I do, Lord?

How have you experienced God this week?

Select one verse or passage from this chapter that was meaningful to you this week, and write it here.

We live in a world of images that deeply influence how we look at life. Choose a picture from this chapter that is meaningful or disturbing to you, and briefly explain why.

Reflecting on what was most meaningful to you from this chapter, respond to one (or more) of these questions in the journal below:

- Who are you, Lord? (an insight into God's character or heart)
- What shall I do, Lord? (an idea for practical application)
- Who shall I be, Lord? (a sense of personal identity)
- Other response?

JOURNAL

SUGGESTED MEMORY VERSE FOR THIS CHAPTER:

GODLY JEALOUSY — HOSEA 2:19-20

I will betroth you to me forever; I will betroth you in righteousness and justice, in love and compassion. I will betroth you in faithfulness, and you will acknowledge the LORD.

41

DIGGING DEEPER

SEXUALITY, SPIRITUALITY, AND JEALOUSY: A SEARCH FOR MEANINGS

Twelve people in their twenties and thirties in a small group were asked this question: "Is jealousy a positive or a negative emotion to you?" All but one said it was negative.

They turned to the only person who viewed jealousy as positive and asked her why. She replied, "Because when my husband stopped being jealous for me, it was the end of our relationship."

During the sexual revolution of the mid-sixties, lots of behaviors long considered to be negative became positive — at least in the popular culture. But there was one significant casualty that went almost unnoticed: jealousy. Jealousy took on an entirely negative face. If you were jealous, people began to think you had a serious problem. The church, for the most part, felt the same way. That small group described above was an adult Sunday school class. Eleven believers said jealousy was bad; only one person said it was good. So which is it? — bad or good?

To make things even more confusing, consider this about God:

> For I, the LORD your God, am a jealous God. (Exodus 20:5)
> For the Lord, whose name is Jealous, is a jealous God. (Exodus 34:14)

If the "good" Lord's name is Jealous, then jealousy can't be all that bad, can it? Yet, it kind of makes God seem schizophrenic — one day merciful, the next day in a jealous rage. Is it really possible to like or trust a jealous God? Is a jealous God safe to be around?

So what's positive about jealousy? Maybe understanding God's jealousy will help us integrate His love with His mercy, holiness, and justice. After all, wasn't Jesus sent to demonstrate the jealous love of God? It really makes you think, doesn't it?

Let's try to connect some dots here. Truth: God created us in His image. Another truth: God created us sexual beings. (It's good to note here that God did have other options. He could easily have made humans capable of asexual reproduction — like earthworms! But He didn't. Why not?) There must be something God wanted us to know about Him that is best "discovered" through our sexuality. Maybe He created us sexual so that we would understand somewhere deep in our beings that He is a jealous God.

Let's pause on that thought. As we said before, we all know that human sexuality is practiced in lots of different forms: heterosexual, homosexual, and bisexual, for starters. People in all of these relationships experience the universal emotion of jealousy. Even though sexual immorality seems acceptable today, jealousy remains a constant.

So in our search for meaning, consider this: a primary meaning of sexuality is that God has created us for relationship with each other. He has also called us to Himself. Godly jealousy is a protective, possessive, delighting, and liberating covering that deals with the issue of shame in relationships. Sometimes we feel vaguely "ashamed" if we aren't in any relationship; we may be jealous (or is it envious?) of friends who are getting married. Somehow we may believe that having a boy/girlfriend or getting married will remove the "stigma" or "shame" of prolonged singleness. And some who are married envy their single friends.

It was godly jealousy that Paul explained symbolically in 2 Corinthians 11:2:

I am jealous for you with a godly jealousy. I promised you to one husband, to Christ, so that I might present you as a pure virgin to him.

It was this same kind of protective, possessive, delighting, godly jealousy that the Beloved sings about in Song of Songs 8:6 when she says:

Place me like a seal over your heart, like a seal on your arm;
>   *for love is as strong as death,*
>   *its jealousy unyielding as the grave.*
>   *It burns like blazing fire,*
>   *like a mighty flame.*

This kind of jealousy in people reflects God's image in us. It expresses itself in cherishing and vigilantly guarding what rightfully belongs to us. Godly jealousy is what burns in the heart of a person whose spouse is having an affair, or in the heart of a parent watching helplessly as his/her child is ensnared by addictions or destructive relationships. This is the positive face of jealousy that has been virtually lost in our culture.

Maybe that's because sin has distorted godly jealousy into something more hostile, distrustful, suspicious, and angry. Worldly jealousy seems driven more by the urge to control the other than by the passion to cherish the other. It's this worldly face of jealousy that Paul spoke of in 1 Corinthians 3:3 (and elsewhere) when he rebukes the Corinthians: "You are still worldly. For since there is jealousy and quarreling among you, are you not worldly? Are you not acting like mere men?" It seems that their jealousy had become overly possessive and an excuse to control others motivated by envy. So does much of the jealousy we see portrayed in the media today.

Remember the lone advocate for jealousy in that small group? She said that when her husband stopped being jealous for her, it spelled the death of their marriage. Well, consider this: What if God stopped being jealous for us? What do you think that would do to our relationship with Him? Often we neglect to thank Him for being jealous for us:

> . . . for cherishing us so much that He is relentlessly protective, possessive, and delighted with us

. . . for fighting for our hearts against all the other gods and idols that compete for
our affection

. . . for not walking out on us, even when we walk out on Him

Now that's the kind of jealous love we all yearn for!

So what does all this talk about jealousy have to do with our sexuality? Well, it is the
miracle of our sexuality that allows us to symbolically and experientially perceive the jealous heart of God for humankind — and for each of us as individuals. When human sexual
relationships are protectively wrapped with the meaning and passion of godly jealousy, then
heterosexual, monogamous, lifetime relationships take on a deeper meaning and point us
to the life-giving relationship offered in Jesus. When the Body of Christ falls in love with the
God who is jealous for us, we can properly delight in the God who delighted in us first! Even
more, we're not as tempted to play games with God — as Israel did in Hosea's day (Hosea
6:1-6) when she acted more like a spiritual prostitute than a devout wife to God. That's when
the exquisite beauty of God's jealous love really shines — as we love being loved by Him and
love loving Him as a devout bride.

In Ezekiel's day, God tried to reclaim the love and devotion of Jerusalem (the Israelite
people) away from their flirtation and fascination with other gods — many of whom demanded
sexual acts as perverted signs of worship. To get through to Jerusalem and show them
the profanity of their choices, God resorted to using the most sexually explicit language in
the Bible (meaning, the prostitution in Ezekiel 16:1-22 and the bestiality in Ezekiel 23:18-21).
After centuries of calling her back to Himself, His divine jealousy compelled Him to punish
Jerusalem for spiritual adultery. After all, what loving husband would feel and do less?

What about today? What will it take for God to pierce our souls numbed with the profanity of our age? The message of God's jealousy for humanity demonstrated in Jesus and
understood through the symbol of sexuality may be the corrective message of hope we long
for. The astounding message of God's jealousy is a very appropriate message for a culture
that is obsessed with sexuality.

The message of God's jealousy is also very good news for all of us who have tasted the
pain of abandonment in our relationships. Did somebody walk out on you who really should
have stayed? Did someone stop fighting for your affection who should have refused to give
up on your relationship? Then cling to the reality that the jealous love of God Himself says
to you:

*I will not in any way fail you nor give you up nor leave you without support. [I will]
not, [I will] not, I will not in any degree leave you helpless nor forsake nor let [you]
down (relax My hold on you)! [Assuredly not!]* (Hebrews 13:5, AMP)

It is no accident that this passionate expression of God's jealousy follows immediately
after His command for us to honor our sexuality:

Let marriage be held in honor (esteemed worthy, precious, of great price, and espe-cially dear) in all things. And thus let the marriage bed be undefiled (kept undis-honored); for God will judge and punish the unchaste [all guilty of sexual vice] and adulterous. (Hebrews 13:4, AMP)

God gifted us with sexuality so that we could appreciate and experience His jealous love for us. And He created us with the capacity for godly jealousy so that we would cherish and protect our closest relationships — especially sexual relationships.

No wonder Satan wants to obliterate any biblical understanding of God's jealous love and replace it with a warped, malicious, envy-driven caricature of the real thing. And no wonder God centrally positioned this truth ("I, the LORD your God, am a jealous God") right in the second commandment (Exodus 20:5). There it is — placed in the Ten Commandments and the Holy of Holies so we would never forget that God loves us jealously. Even though it is important for us to know and experience God's jealous love, don't expect to find the word "jealousy" everywhere in the Bible. Actually, you won't find many New Testament refer-ences to jealousy, other than the few we've quoted in this article. Like the word "trinity," the concept of God's jealous love is embedded throughout Scripture, although the term is rarely used.

However, when you read the teachings of Jesus (see Luke 11–18), you just know that He had the jealous love of the Father in mind. Emotionally, these passages seem to echo with the cries of a discarded Lover who seeks to arouse some remnant of jealousy within His chosen Beloved. Historically, the Beloved represented Israel. It's the same Israel who Paul appeals to by saying,

Salvation has come to the Gentiles to make Israel envious. . . . I am talking to you Gentiles . . . in the hope that I may somehow arouse my own people to envy and save some of them. (Romans 11:11-14)

Here are a few other words from Jesus that reflect the jealous heart of God without actu-ally using the word jealousy:

O Jerusalem, Jerusalem, you who kill the prophets and stone those sent to you, how often I have longed to gather your children together, as a hen gathers her chicks under her wings, but you were not willing! Look, your house is left to you desolate. (Luke 13:34-35)

No servant can serve two masters. Either he will hate the one and love the other, or he will be devoted to the one and despise the other. You cannot serve both God and Money! (Luke 16:13)

It is possible to remove jealousy from sexuality — for a while. But not forever. Jealousy is like glue. It binds us to each other. It can reveal the preciousness within a relationship. It can symbolically draw us back to God.

Of course not all Scripture is about God's jealousy. But if we remove or even minimize the centrality of God's jealousy in relating to His people, we have lost something that we desperately long for as sexual beings: to be jealously, protectively, and exclusively cherished by the Lover of our souls whose very name is Jealous.

CHAPTER 3
MASCULINITY AND FEMININITY: WHAT'S THE DIFFERENCE?

Danica enjoyed being a girl until about age twelve. Then everything seemed to change. The boys seemed to have a better deal. They had more freedom. She wanted freedom from being a female. As she began to dress and act more boyish, she noticed that the boys were slowly treating her as one of the guys.

For the next fifteen years, this strategy for dealing with gender differences worked pretty well for her. As for sex . . . that was never a problem; it was like any other sweaty full contact sport where you win some and you lose some.

But then the playing field began to change. Some of her friends got married and started having children. Something new began stirring inside Danica. She began to sense the mystery of being a woman, of not being one of the guys. Was there something really good and exciting about being a woman that she had missed earlier? Was it too late for her to learn how to embrace her femininity and enjoy being a woman?

Can you relate to Danica's story? Or does this remind you of anyone? *Explain.*

Gender is a reality and a more fundamental reality than sex. Sex is, in fact, merely the adaptation to organic life of a fundamental polarity that divides all created beings. Female sex is simply one of the things which has feminine gender; there are many others and Masculine and Feminine meet us on planes of reality where male and female would be simply meaningless. . . . The male and female of organic creatures are rather faint and blurred reflections of masculine and feminine. . . . Their reproductive functions, their differences in shape and size partly exhibit, partly also confuse and misrepresent, the real polarity.

— C. S. LEWIS, *THAT HIDEOUS STRENGTH*

PAUƧE 1_EXPLORING WHAT GOD ƧAYƧ

Your gender identity has been a core part of your true identity ever since the moment you were conceived. Probably the first words spoken about you were either "It's a boy!" or "It's a girl!" The Bible reveals that God designed us with gender as a gift — and that He wants us to experience our gender as "very good."

Do you usually view your gender as more of a gift or more of a curse, or something else? *Explain.*

As you reflect on your gender as God's gift to you, what emotions surface within you?

In your opinion, what is positive about masculinity?

What is negative about masculinity?

In your opinion, what is positive about femininity?

What is negative about femininity?

In the introductory story, Danica had some questions and struggles regarding her gender. How secure and comfortable do you feel now in your gender identity as a man or a woman?

As a woman, do you enjoy your femininity? As a man, do you enjoy your masculinity? Why or why not?

PAU∫E 2_EXPLORING YOUR REALITY

Have you ever wanted to ask God, "What in the world were you thinking when you made us male and female?" The Bible records not one but two stories about God's original creation of the human race. Each story provides a slightly different perspective on God's intent in creating us in His image to be male and female. After reading each story, reflect on key verses.

ADAM AND EVE'∫ COMMONALITIE∫ (GENE∫I∫ 1:26-31)

From this first account, what do you observe about the creation of humans? <u>Notice particularly what man and woman shared in common</u>.

verse 26

verse 27

verse 28

verses 29-30

verse 31

What do you think it means to be made in God's image?

Why do you think God chose to reflect His image through two unique beings — not just one?

Why do you think God gave the privilege of ruling over nature to both man and woman?

Why do you think God called His creation of male and female "very good"? What's so "good" and "glorious" about it? (Compare with Psalm 8:5-8.)

By creating a person like Adam yet very unlike Adam, God provided the possibility of a profound unity that otherwise would have been impossible. There is a different kind of unity enjoyed by the joining of diverse counterparts than is enjoyed by joining two things just alike. When we all sing the same melody line it is called unison, which means "one sound." But when we unite diverse lines of soprano and alto and tenor and bass, we call it harmony; and everyone who has an ear to hear knows that something deeper in us is touched by great harmony than by mere unison. So God made a woman and not another man.

— JOHN PIPER, *DESIRING GOD*

ADAM AND EVE'S UNIQUE GOD-DESIGN (GENESIS 2:15-25)

From this second account of the same event, what do you observe about the creation of humans? Notice particularly <u>what was distinct about the man and the woman.</u>

verses 15-17

verse 18   *NOTE: This verse contains two Hebrew words to describe the woman:* ezer kenegdo *meaning "helper along-side." These terms are used elsewhere in the Old Testament to describe God Himself. They are variously translated into English as "suitable companion; helper as his counterpoint; helper as his partner; helper who is suitable, adapted, complementary, fit, right for him; helper suited to his needs," etc.*

verses 19-20   *NOTE: Having been created first, Adam lived "alone" for a time, focusing on the work God gave him to do. This suggests that part of God-designed masculinity includes the power to act, do, lead, initiate, work, and encounter the world with courage.*

verses 21-23   *NOTE: Having been created second, Eve stepped into life in the context of human relationship. She was also uniquely empowered to carry and bring new life into the world. This suggests that part of God-designed femininity includes strong relational capacity, including nurturing, responding, and intuitive understanding of others.*

verses 24-25

How do you think Adam and Eve's unique God-design helped and complemented each other?

ADAM AND EVE'S FALL (GENESIS 3:1-24)

Up to this point in the story, Scripture implies that Adam and Eve enjoyed the beautiful "dance" of gender — characterized by joy, unity, partnership, moral innocence, freedom, equality, pleasure, beauty, complementing each other, and not a trace of shame over their gender or sexuality. That is, until the great deceiver brought evil into their world and turned their dance with God and each other into a deadly duel.

From this continuing account of their Fall, what do you observe about the impact of their sin on their identity and experience as male and female?

verses 1-5   *NOTE: Satan tempted Eve by getting her wanting to be like someone else — to be what she was not.*

In what ways do you still want to be like someone else, other than who you are?

verses 6-7   *NOTE: Adam seems to have been with Eve when she was tempted.*

What part (if any) do you think Adam's silence and passivity played in the Fall?

What part have you seen men's silence and passivity play in the world today?

Consider the following quote. Are there any ways in which you feel ashamed or inadequate about your masculinity or femininity? Can you trace those feelings back to any specific events, comments, failures, rejections, or medical issues from your past? *Explain.*

Shameful nakedness conveyed a fracturing of humanity's original unity with God and with each other. Adam in his nakedness hid from God. This tendency toward concealment applies to people's relationship with God and with one another. Recognizing the other's nakedness produces conflict. Full disclosure of the self is no longer possible. Having complemented one another well in Eden, Adam and Eve braced for mutual brokenness outside the garden.

— ANDREW COMISKEY, *STRENGTH IN WEAKNESS*

verses 8-13

verses 14-16

How do you see God's curse on the serpent impacting the lives of women from Eve up until today? (verses 14-15)

What consequences do you think the Fall has had on women's God-given relational strength, inclining women to search for their identity in their relationships in unhealthy ways, especially in their relationships with men and with other women? (verse 16)

verses 17-19

How do you see God's curse on the ground affecting the daily lives of men from Adam up until today?

What effect do you think this consequence has had on men's God-given strength in "doing" and taking initiative, inclining men to find their identity in their work in unhealthy ways?

What effect has this consequence had on men's relationships with women, and with other men?

verse 20

verses 21-24

Follow the tracks of pain into the lives of man and woman. How will each experience pain differently in their new fallen and broken worlds?

What does this suggest about the unique design of man and woman?

The Fall impacted the relationship between Adam and Eve in a way that we replay in our own lives today. Sin challenges inspired complementarity. Subject now to the effects of evil, men and women are capable of bruising each other. Our respective strengths — woman's relational sensibility, man's power to act — threaten to create discord rather than the wholeness God intended.

— ANDREW COMISKEY, *STRENGTH IN WEAKNESS*

How do man's sense of futility in his work and woman's sense of pain in her relationships impact the other gender?

Consider that pride and envy played a significant part in the Fall. How might God's consequences to Adam and Eve serve to bring humility to both of them?

How might these consequences also be an act of grace?

PAUSE 3_COMING ALIVE TO GOD AND OTHERS

MALE AND FEMALE REFLECTING THE IMAGE OF GOD

God created us male and female in His image. We get a picture of who God is and what He is like through glimpses of masculinity and femininity. According to these passages, God is like whom?

ISAIAH 66:13   A mother comforting her child.

PSALM 103:13

PSALM 131:2-3

PROVERBS 3:12

ISAIAH 62:5

ISAIAH 66:7-11

God has revealed Himself as triune — three persons in one. Since God also "in the image of God he created them; male and female he created them," (Genesis 1:27, NLT). Since God patterned us after Himself, what connections might there be between God's nature and our masculinity and femininity?

MALE AND FEMALE DOING GOOD WORKS

In addition to reflecting God's image, consider what this verse says about God's purpose in designing us as He did.

> *EPHESIANS 2:10. For we are God's workmanship, created in Christ Jesus to do good works, which God prepared in advance for us to do.*

How might your gender be an important factor in doing the works God prepared in advance for you to do?

*Words can only partially describe **the mystery of God's image embedded within masculinity and femininity**. And yet our souls respond to these differences as well as to the commonalities between genders. This **dance** continues for a lifetime!*

To unpack the mystery of God's image embedded within masculinity and femininity, think about the metaphor of dancing — or skating — with a partner. What happens when both lead at the same time? Does the one leading have to be the better dancer?

Do you think relationships between men and women resemble a dance? If so, how?

It's pretty obvious that masculinity is not about muscles and being macho, any more than femininity is about make-up and manicures. So, from your study of God's design of gender at creation, <u>what are some central tendencies and things to celebrate about being masculine and feminine</u>?

MASCULINE	FEMININE

PRAYER PAUSE

No matter how distorted God's image has become in us, He who created our gender can also redeem and restore what is essential and true about our femininity and masculinity. He longs to bless us as His sons and His daughters. Ask God to reveal what you may not be aware of as you look at your gender issues and realities.

PAUƧE 4_JOURNEYING FORWARD

ACTS 22:8,10.   Who are you, Lord?
What shall I do, Lord?

How have you experienced God this week?

Select one verse or passage from this chapter that was meaningful to you this week, and write it here.

We live in a world of images that deeply influence how we look at life. Choose a picture from this chapter that is meaningful or disturbing to you, and briefly explain why.

Reflecting on what was most meaningful to you from this chapter, respond to one (or more) of these questions in the journal on the next page:

- Who are you, Lord? (an insight into God's character or heart)
- What shall I do, Lord? (an idea for practical application)
- Who shall I be, Lord? (a sense of personal identity)
- Other response?

JOURNAL

MALE AND FEMALE — GENESIS 1:27

So God created man in his own image, in the image of God he created him; male and female he created them.

DIGGING DEEPER

Tendencies of Masculine and Feminine Sexual Activity Through Symbolically Linking Biological Functions

	MASCULINE TENDENCIES	**FEMININE TENDENCIES**
Foreplay	**Attracts** with physical and inner strength and social prestige Attracted to the **sensual pleasure** and honor of being accepted and trusted	**Attracts** with physical and inner beauty and social prestige Attracted to **sensual pleasure** and the intimacy of a possessive bond
Intercourse	**Penetrates** with respectful love	**Surrounds** with embracing love
Climax	**Surrenders** with honor	**Surrenders** with trust
Ejaculation	**Gives**	**Receives**
Conception	**Sacrifices** sperm and Defines the baby	**Selects** the sperm
Gestation	**Protects** the mother and child	**Develops** the child
Birth	**An Empathetic** partner	**Bears** a new life in pain

These dynamics of gender differences in sexual acts encourage humility before each other and God.

Does sexual symbolism help you appreciate God's mysterious design? *Explain.*

CHAPTER 4
MANHOOD AND WOMANHOOD:
HOW CAN I EMBRACE MY GENDER?

Antonio was mostly okay being a male until high school. But when his friends slowly separated into cliques, he just didn't fit their stereotypes. Besides, he didn't like being categorized. He seemed to fit everywhere and nowhere.

When he was in the ninth grade, his father left the family. So Antonio was thrust into the role of helping provide for his younger brother and sisters. Often he just felt powerless. He didn't make enough money. He didn't meet his mom's expectations and emotional needs. He didn't feel like he really fit in with the guys. And he didn't have a lot of confidence relating to women. He worried that he just didn't have what it takes to be enough for any woman. But he definitely was a male. He just wasn't clear what that meant.

Now in their early twenties, Antonio and his girlfriend are running into both their own and each other's gender issues. Intuitively they sense that they need each other. And they are experiencing new aspects of themselves coming alive as they explore what it means to live out of their masculinity and femininity.

Can you relate to Antonio's situation? Or does this remind you of anyone? Explain.

*But this is not the end of the story. God not only created us, but **He also restores us to be men and women who reflect His image**. As we identify with Jesus' death and resurrection, He raises up our true selves. God wants to make us secure as men and women. He wants us to be strong and empowered men and women, passionate for Him and His people. When we are secure as men and women, our passion for Him and others is strengthened and purified.*

— CATHY MORRILL, *SOLUTIONS: RELATIONAL HEALING FOR THE NEXT GENERATION*

PAUSE 1_EXPLORING WHAT GOD SAYS

The Bible never directly uses the words "gender" or "masculinity" or "femininity." However, the Bible does offer us many stories where couples (most married, some not) depict traits of masculinity and femininity as God designed it to be. Others demonstrate what happens when sin distorts God's design into false, worldly — or blatantly destructive — expressions of manhood and womanhood.

All of the couples in these stories were married. The Bible contains very few references to stories about unmarried people, perhaps for cultural reasons. However, the traits that characterize masculinity and femininity (mature and immature) appear just as much in unmarried people as they do in married people. Whether you are married or not, you will relate as a man or as a woman to others of the opposite gender all through your life.

What can we learn about <u>mature masculinity and femininity</u> from these biblical couples?

READ THEIR STORY FROM:	HOW DID THE MAN OFFER ASPECTS OF HIS MATURE MASCU- LINITY <u>FOR HER OR OTHERS?</u>	HOW DID THE WOMAN OFFER ASPECTS OF HER MATURE FEMI- NINITY <u>FOR HIM OR OTHERS?</u>
SONG OF SOLOMON	SONG OF SOLOMON 1:15; 2:15; 4:9; 6:5; and others	SOLOMON'S SHULAMMITE BRIDE 1:6; 2:16; 5:10; 7:10; 8:67; and others
EPHESIANS 5:21-33	HUSBAND	WIFE

READ THEIR STORY FROM:	HOW DID THE MAN OFFER ASPECTS OF HIS MATURE MASCU-LINITY FOR HER OR OTHERS?	HOW DID THE WOMAN OFFER ASPECTS OF HER MATURE FEMI-NINITY FOR HIM OR OTHERS?
(Optional Study)	JOSEPH	MARY
MATTHEW 1:18-25		
MATTHEW 2:19-23		
LUKE 1:26-38		

MALE AND FEMALE CONTRIBUTING INNER STRENGTH AND BEAUTY

READ 1 Peter 3:3-9, where Peter counsels husbands and wives on how to bless — and be blessed by — one another across genders. (Suggestion: Read these verses in several different versions of the Bible.)

verses 3-5   *NOTE: When Peter encouraged women to be "quiet," he wasn't asking them to be silent or untalkative or introverted, but to be peaceful inwardly. Verse 4 in the Amplified Bible says: "But let it be the inward adorning and beauty of the hidden person of the heart, with the incorruptible and unfading charm of a gentle and peaceful spirit, which [is not anxious or wrought up, but] is very precious in the sight of God."*

What qualities do you think characterize a woman with "inner beauty"?

verse 7   *NOTE: Paul's reference to women as "weaker" refers to their sheer physical strength, not their moral stamina, strength of character, or mental capacity.*

What qualities do you think characterize a mature, masculine man?

verses 8-9

What inner qualities should all followers of Christ — men and women, married and unmarried — live out in their relationships?

Look at the memory verses for this chapter in Pause 4, taken from 1 Peter 3.

Men, would you want your girlfriend or wife to be like the woman in verse 4?

Women, would you want your boyfriend or husband to be like the man in verse 7? Explain.

PAU/E 2_EXPLORING YOUR REALITY

In your first ten to fifteen years of life, your sense of being a boy or a girl was influenced — for good or for bad — by parental models, TV shows and movies, video games, interactions with your peers, advertising and fashion, significant adults, etc.

Reflect for a moment on your first fifteen years, and describe how these influences (or others) shaped your sense of being male or female.

How did your awareness of your gender change during your teen years and early adulthood? Consider both your enjoyment and your pains surrounding your growth as a young man or young woman.

Think about how masculinity and femininity are portrayed in the media. How do you think it stacks up against what you see in the Bible?

Since we live in a fallen world, how have you seen masculinity misused?

How have you seen femininity misused?

How do you think these events (of misuse) have influenced the way you view your gender — and the opposite gender?

In your experience, are the dynamics between men and women more like a beautiful dance or a deadly duel? Explain.

(NOTE: In case you haven't thought much about duels, that's when two people oppose each other in destructive ways, and it doesn't end until one is wounded — or dead!)

PAUSE 3_COMING ALIVE TO GOD AND OTHERS

What can we learn about fallen, unhealthy, immature masculinity and femininity from these biblical couples?

READ THEIR STORY FROM:	HOW DID HE USE HIS INNER (OR PHYSICAL) STRENGTH AGAINST HER OR OTHERS?	HOW DID SHE USE HER INNER (OR PHYSICAL) STRENGTH AGAINST HIM OR OTHERS?
JUDGES 16	SAMSON	DELILAH
1 KINGS 16:29-34 1 KINGS 18:1–19:9 1 KINGS 21 2 KINGS 9:30–10:17	KING AHAB	JEZEBEL

READ THEIR STORY FROM:	HOW DID HE USE HIS INNER (OR PHYSICAL) STRENGTH AGAINST HER OR OTHERS?	HOW DID SHE USE HER INNER (OR PHYSICAL) STRENGTH AGAINST HIM OR OTHERS?
HOSEA 1:1–3:3	HOSEA	GOMER
1 SAMUEL 25	NABAL	ABIGAIL
(Optional Study) ESTHER 2:17-18 ESTHER 4–8 ESTHER 9:29-32	XERXES	ESTHER

LET'S SUMMARIZE. From all of the passages you studied, and your own observations, how would you describe:

MATURE MASCULINITY	FALLEN MASCULINITY
	Abusive and macho Emotionless workaholic Other?

MATURE FEMININITY	FALLEN FEMININITY
	Overdependent on other people, especially men Manipulative and controlling Other?

In your opinion, how can men (married and single) offer what is truest and best about their masculinity to their families, friends, and society?

In your opinion, how can women (married and single) offer what is truest and best about their femininity to their families, friends, and society?

Gender differences can lead to humility, humiliation, or to arrogant pride. What tends to be your experience?

____ Humiliation says, I feel inferior and inadequate because I can't do what they (the opposite gender) do. I just don't feel good enough.
____ Pride says, I can do things better than they can. I really don't need them.
____ Humility says, I wasn't designed to do everything they can do. So I see my need for them, and am grateful for their presence in my life.

In what ways do you have deep respect for males and females? How do you show that respect?

Are there ways in which you disrespect males and/or females? Explain.

Have you felt insecure about being a man or a woman? If so, how?

What is one way you want to grow in your identity and security as a man or woman, and in your celebration and respect for masculinity and femininity?

PRAYER PAUSE

In taking your issues of gender to the Lord, you can pray something like this[1]:

Father, I am tired of fighting with my own insecurity. I want to feel secure and adequate and sure of myself as a man (woman). Sometimes I confuse what others say I should be like with who I really am. I've tried to act confident when I really wasn't. I confess that sometimes I've looked to other things but not to you for my gender identity. I want to put it all down at the cross now, especially how I see myself as a man (woman). I want to offer my strength and beauty to others for their good instead of using my masculinity (femininity) against them for my own gratification. I cry out for your touch! Father, I really need your affirmation and blessing on me as a man (woman). Please come and strengthen me from the inside out to be a man (woman) who loves and reflects you.

Now continue praying in your own words. . . .

[1] These prayers are adapted from *SOULutions* by Wendy Coy Cathy Morrill, Desert Stream Press (2000), p. 83.

And the Father might reply something like this:

> *My Son, my Daughter, from the beginning of time, I have called you my own. I called you to reveal me in your manhood, your womanhood. I never lost sight of the real you, no matter how dark or difficult life became for you. Through the blood of my Son, I made a way for you to be united with the good gift of your gender, your body, and all the unique ways I designed you to reveal me in your personality. Let me father you now. Don't let doubt or shame cripple your sense of wonder and respect for your gender — or that of others. Turn away from self-rejection and self-hatred into the warmth of my favor upon your personhood. Don't rely on your childish feelings, but rather on my unfailing love and acceptance. As often as you have to, give to my Son all the shame and judgment you still struggle with in regard to your gender and body. Let His victory be yours. Abide in my approval and delight over you. And then live out the glory of your true masculinity (femininity) in the humble way you love, respect, and offer yourself to others — all as a reflection of my glory.*

Now respond to God's blessing in your own way. . . .

PAUSE 4_JOURNEYING FORWARD

ACTS 22:8,10.   Who are you, Lord?
                 What shall I do, Lord?

How have you experienced God this week?

Select one verse or passage from this chapter that was meaningful to you this week, and write it here.

We live in a world of images that deeply influence how we look at life. Choose a picture from this chapter that is meaningful or disturbing to you, and briefly explain why.

Reflecting on what was most meaningful to you from this chapter, respond to one (or more) of these questions in the journal on the next page:

- Who are you, Lord? (an insight into God's character or heart)
- What shall I do, Lord? (an idea for practical application)
- Who shall I be, Lord? (a sense of personal identity)
- Other response?

JOURNAL

SUGGESTED MEMORY VERSE FOR THIS CHAPTER:

HUSBANDS AND WIVES
MEN AND WOMEN — 1 PETER 3:4,7

You should clothe yourselves instead with the beauty that comes from within, the unfading beauty of a gentle and quiet spirit, which is so precious to God. . . .

In the same way, you husbands must give honor to your wives. Treat your wife with understanding as you live together. She may be weaker than you are, but she is your equal partner in God's gift of new life. Treat her as you should so your prayers will not be hindered. (NLT)

DIGGING DEEPER

SUMMARY

Believers have different perspectives on what defines mature masculinity and femininity. Some focus on central tendencies of masculine and feminine from creation, while others focus on the differing roles of male and female in marriage and in the church. In these last two chapters, we've tried simply to point you to some key passages and invite you to draw your own conclusions. We wanted to give you an opportunity to:

1. Explore a few aspects of gender.
2. Glimpse some of God's attributes reflected by mature masculinity and femininity.
3. Explore some of the central tendencies of masculinity and femininity.
4. Learn from biblical couples what true masculinity and true femininity (as God designed it to be) looks like. Also learn from those couples what it looks like when sin twists God's design into various distorted and false expressions of masculinity and femininity. At its best you observed the graceful "dance" of gender; at its worst you observed the destructive "duel" between the genders.
5. Embrace the mystery of God's creation of gender wrapped in strength and beauty offered for others' well-being, and investigate why God called this mystery "very good." This celebration of gender is available equally to those who are married and those who are not.
6. Grow in humility, thankfulness, and respect for men and women, including yourself, and for God who made them both.

MATURE MASCULINITY AND MATURE FEMININITY

In his book *Falling Forward*, author Craig Lockwood states that mature masculinity:

- Refuses to be reduced to raw sexual desire in relationships. Instead, maturity involves being aware of the woman's deeper, personal needs.
- Is not mastered by the threat of woman's differences. The energy of her sensuality, the power of her emotions, and her capacity to reject him give way, through healing, to the masculine desire to protect her.
- Does not look down on women condescendingly, or abuse his power through the use of self-aggrandizing authoritarianism. Instead, he leads them as fellow heirs of Christ, whom he prizes and honors, treating them as extensions of his own body.
- Does not confuse the sexual relationship with emotional intimacy. Sexuality, therefore, takes second place to friendship and communion of the soul.

From everything you've learned about biblical expressions of gender, make several similar statements of your own about femininity:

Mature femininity . . .

Mature femininity . . .

Mature femininity . . .

CHAPTER 5
SEXUALITY: HOW DO I HANDLE PLEASURES, HURTS, AND LUSTS?

Several years ago I visited a nearby university campus to speak to a student group. During my talk I briefly mentioned God's desires for our sexual well-being. Immediately after the talk, a female student rushed up to me and said, "We have to talk . . . outside!" So we stepped into the hall, and she started her story.

"My boyfriend and I are believers. At the beginning of our relationship, we both committed ourselves to sexual purity as God's best for us. But then, one night we crossed our boundaries into petting and soon had sex. We felt terrible and resolved never to do that again."

"So how's it going?" I asked her, fairly sure that I knew the answer already.

"That's the problem. Now we do it every time we're together. We just can't stop. And it's ruining our relationship. What can we do?" she pleaded.

Tears came to my eyes, understanding how difficult and complex their struggles were.

Then she added, "Oh, one more thing — I know you don't know this, but my boyfriend is in the Bible study group you lead at your school."

That really got my attention. I knew that canned answers wouldn't help this couple.

What part of this couple's story (if any) can you connect with?

The problem is not that we talk about sex. The problem is how we talk about sex. So much of what we say about sex is wrong, deceptive, distorted, misleading. This matters, because the way we talk about sex reflects and forms the way we think about, and ultimately the way we practice, sex. Much of what we say about sex in public is, simply, false. And when we tell falsehoods about sex, and listen to falsehoods about sex, we wind up living falsehoods about sex.

— LAUREN WINNER, *REAL SEX: THE NAKED TRUTH ABOUT CHASTITY*

Ours is a sex-saturated society. Beverage commercials, TV shows, video games, perfume ads, the emerging world of cyberporn — it feels like sex is everywhere. Sexual innocence in children disappears at an early age. The sexual behavior bell curve has been expanded to include homosexuality, bisexuality, metasexuality, polygamy, orgy worship, and bestiality alongside the biblical ideals of virginity and monogamous, lifetime heterosexual marriage relationships.

You'd think that having so many sexual options would clear up our confusion. Instead, it just makes us more confused. Where are the boundaries to be drawn? Who determines the boundaries? What happens when we cross them? And why have boundaries, anyway?

God designed us as spiritual creatures wrapped in sexual bodies. Sex is about jealous love . . . and about beauty, power, and authenticity. Sexuality is a beautiful and powerful part of who He created us to be. So it makes sense that God would have given us a guide to sexual wisdom to help us enjoy our sexual gifts in ways that fulfill our souls — not cheapen them. These boundaries and the authority behind them serve to protect our hearts and the well-being of our relationships.

PAUSE 1_EXPLORING WHAT GOD SAYS

The apostle Paul wrote in 1 Corinthians 10:12-13, "So, if you think you are standing firm, be careful that you don't fall! No temptation has seized you except what is common to man. And God is faithful; he will not let you be tempted beyond what you can bear. But when you are tempted, he will also provide a way out so that you can stand up under it." Paul understood God as the One who shows us this "way of escape." It is an escape to inner life rather than what could bring our souls death. In Scripture, God also provides us with many stories of people who both stood and fell in respect to how they used their sexuality for good or for evil. Let's look at two case studies on this topic.

CASE STUDY: DAVID AND BATHSHEBA
(2 SAMUEL 11–12)

QUICK BACKGROUND: When David committed adultery with Bathsheba and followed it up with conspiracy, deceit, murder, and cover-up, he was most certainly not living life well — sexually or otherwise. So why study David's story? Because it was David who showed us how to respond to moral failure *after* it happens — and that is where many of us in our sexualized culture find ourselves sooner or later. So when we have failed to take "the way of escape" from temptations that are oh-so-common to man (that includes women), David's story provides important keys to repentance and restoration. Think of it as an illustration of sexuality redeemed.

READ 2 SAMUEL 11. List several of the sins David committed.

What lies do you imagine David may have told himself in order to justify or give himself permission to commit those sins?

READ 2 SAMUEL 12:13-14, which is David's response after he was caught and accused. Also scan PSALM 51 which David wrote in response to his sin.

How did David respond inwardly and outwardly to the Lord's rebuke through Nathan?

What were the consequences of David's sins, both immediately, throughout his life, and for later generations?

CASE STUDY: THE RAPE OF TAMAR
(2 SAMUEL 13:1-21,26)

What happens in our hearts and souls when we cross the sexual boundaries God has set for our own good? To find out, read the tragic story of Amnon (King David's son) who raped his sister Tamar. He did much more than devalue her: He devastated and destroyed her. Feel her pain as she cried out, "Where could I go in my shame? Where could I get rid of my disgrace?" (verse 13, NLT). She ended up spending the rest of her life holed up, "bitter" and "desolate" (verse 20, NLT). But it didn't end there. This sexual crime devastated Amnon, too — as well as David and his entire family.

After reading the story, notice what harm came from Amnon's sexual choices.

♦ Have you ever despaired, like Tamar, that you would never be able to get rid of shame and disgrace linked with your sexuality? If so, describe how it felt.

♦ How, if at all, has the pain of rape or incest impacted you or someone you know?

The cross is the one place where misogyny [the hatred of women] can find its end. Regardless of its expression — be it abuse, abandonment or a woman's self-hatred — Jesus died to bear the sin of misogyny. The crucified One answers the laments of the Tamar's everywhere as they cry out, "Where could I get rid of my disgrace?" One must look no further than the place of great exchange — the cross, where God bears disgrace and grants women holy honor instead.

— ANDREW COMISKEY, *STRENGTH IN WEAKNESS*

From either of these two stories, what did you notice about boundaries being broken, or about violating godly jealous love?

Summarize below any principles or practical strategies you learned from these two stories that can help you live well sexually.

HOW TO AVOID SEXUAL IMMORALITY	HOW TO RESPOND TO MY OWN MORAL FAILURE

PAUSE 2_EXPLORING YOUR REALITY

Without trust nothing lasting is built into a relationship. Allowing for a period of life devoted to courtship without sex is the best gift two people in love could claim for themselves. It is the heart of Romance.

— PAULA RINEHART, *SEX AND THE SOUL OF A WOMAN*

If a dating or engaged couple decides to keep their relationship sexually pure, how do you think that choice would impact their sense of romance?

If you are struggling with any aspect of your sexuality, where could you turn? In addition to God, which of your friends or family do you believe would offer you trusted confidentiality, biblical wisdom, and an environment of grace where you could safely process this issue? Write their names here.

What about you? How would you respond if a friend shared his/her sexual struggles and asked for help? How gracefully do you think you could honestly respond?

What nonsexual needs do people try to fulfill through inappropriate sexual behavior?

In what ways (if any) have you been affected negatively or put down because of your gender?

PRAYER PAUSE

Have you ever had a conversation with God about your sexual longings? Consider all you have to gain by asking God to speak into these realities in your life. Some time this week, try it and see what happens.

Sexual hurts often come in the form of gender bias. At a minor level, we've all heard "dumb blonde" and "clueless male" jokes. We've watched the daytime talk shows and sitcoms turn disrespect for both genders into crass entertainment. But gender bias can have devastating consequences on both men and women — and it appears in the social patterns and legal systems of virtually every culture of the world. Here are some ways that women — and also men — are devalued:

- Sexual abuse
- Prostitution
- Sexual harassment
- Sexual stereotyping
- Pornography
- Sexual assault
- Derogatory comments
- Sexual unfaithfulness in marriage
- Incest
- Rape and molesting
- Gender discrimination
- Sex slavery
- Other?

THE TERMS FOR GENDER BIAS ARE:

MISOGYNY: the dishonor or disrespect (or hatred) of women and femininity
MISANDRY: the dishonor or disrespect (or hatred) of men and masculinity

In the SECOND column, write some ways that women and the feminine way of being are devalued or disrespected.

In the THIRD column, write some ways that men and the masculine way of being are devalued or disrespected.

	WOMEN ARE DEVALUED . . .	MEN ARE DEVALUED . . .
BY CULTURAL PRACTICES AND ATTITUDES		
IN THE MEDIA		
BY MEN	• "Dumb blonde" jokes	• Ridiculing artistic, nonathletic guys as "sissies" or worse • Measuring masculinity by how much they can drink
BY WOMEN	• Dumping their girlfriends for a guy • Limiting career dreams because she's "just a woman"	• "Clueless male" jokes

PAUSE 3_COMING ALIVE TO GOD AND OTHERS

What we focus on will significantly influence how well we handle our sexual desires.

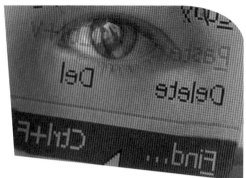

> *2 TIMOTHY 2:22. Run from anything that stimulates youthful lusts. Instead, pursue righteous living, faithfulness, love, and peace. Enjoy the companionship of those who call on the Lord with pure hearts.* (NLT)

To help you "avoid lust" and enjoy the opposite gender "with pure hearts," what is one thing in your life you believe you should "run from" and one thing you should "pursue"?

How might it help us to "flee" from lust if we pursued deepening our respect for the opposite gender?

Jesus had a wonderful ministry of mercy to sexually active people. As you read these two stories, <u>write your observations of how Jesus treated sexually permissive people</u>.

OBSERVATIONS FROM LUKE 7:36-50

OBSERVATIONS FROM JOHN 8:1-11

> *Jesus caught this woman (see John 8) in the place where everyone else would throw her away — the place of her sin and shame. But he takes her by the hand and leads her to freedom. . . . Jesus does not turn away. He steps right in to the mess we have made and offers us not another stone of condemnation but, of all things, MERCY. . . . Out of this place where we have been loved in our shame, we come to know ourselves as women [and men] worthy of love. And this love changes everything.*
>
> — PAULA RINEHART, *SEX AND THE SOUL OF A WOMAN*

Summarize how sexually permissive people responded to Jesus. Why do you think this was so?

How do you respond to Jesus' love and truth regarding sexuality?

In these stories, Jesus is both tough on sin and tender toward people. What would it look like for you to imitate Jesus in this area? How can we show love to people who are practicing sexuality in forms that deny the original design found in the Bible?

♦ If you could find healing in one aspect of your sexuality, what would you like it to be?

What changes, if any, do you need to make in the way you view and treat men and women as sexual beings?

IN CLOSING

Each of us has a sexual history. Some parts may be sweet and innocent; other parts may be confusing or shameful to you. But every part is within the reach of God's mercy. This is what the power of the Gospel is for! In the next chapter we'll consider more on living well as a sexual being.

Of course, there is a difference between struggling with a sexual behavior and being "addicted" to it. If you have tried and tried on your own to stop a particular behavior, but failed, it's probably time to consult a trusted friend or counselor. Also consider the resources in the *Digging Deeper* section at the end of this chapter.

PAUSE 4_JOURNEYING FORWARD

ACTS 22:8,10.   Who are you, Lord?
What shall I do, Lord?

How have you experienced God this week?

Select one verse or passage from this chapter that was meaningful to you this week, and write it here.

We live in a world of images that deeply influence how we look at life. Choose a picture from this chapter that is meaningful or disturbing to you, and briefly explain why.

Reflecting on what was most meaningful to you from this chapter, respond to one (or more) of these questions in the journal on the next page:

- Who are you, Lord? (an insight into God's character or heart)
- What shall I do, Lord? (an idea for practical application)
- Who shall I be, Lord? (a sense of personal identity)
- Other response?

JOURNAL

SUGGESTED MEMORY VERSE FOR THIS CHAPTER:

PROTECTING SEXUALITY — 2 TIMOTHY 2:22

Run from anything that stimulates youthful lusts. Instead, pursue righteous living, faithfulness, love, and peace. Enjoy the companionship of those who call on the Lord with pure hearts. (NLT)

94

DIGGING DEEPER

OTHER ISSUES RELATED TO SEXUALITY

Any authentic exploration of the topic of sexuality inevitably opens up a whole can of worms — other related topics that you may have questions about. Topics like sexual abuse, abortion, rape, homosexuality, different forms of sexual addictions, etc. They are facts of life. And some of them might also be huge personal issues for you.

There's no way we can explore these topics in depth (or even superficially) in this Bible study. But we don't want to dodge any issues that might be blocking your journey into spiritual healing and wholeness.

So here's a way forward: Below you'll find a list of some issues that can negatively impact our ability to live well as sexual beings. It isn't exhaustive by any means. But it's a way of saying "we feel your pain." Perhaps none of these are personal issues for you. Or you may feel overwhelmed, ashamed, or hopeless about one of these issues. But be assured: not one of these issues is too big or too difficult or too messy for your Father to deal with. He can bring healing and freedom to you as He has done for many others. He wants you to talk with Him about what's happened to you and how it is affecting your life, soul, and relationships today.

For each issue, we'll simply make a brief comment and suggest resources that might help you explore the specific issue deeper, both from a biblical viewpoint and also for practical help. These are also resources that may help you minister to others. We suggest that you selectively acquire some of these materials over time.

Last, we hope your small group environment is becoming a safe place where you can bring up issues without fear of condemnation or gossip. At any age, a follower of Christ needs relationships of trust and environments of grace so he/she doesn't have to hide struggles. But don't feel compelled to share with a group or anyone else what your heart needs to keep private for now. For persistent problems, please find a mature believer or counselor whom you can trust to walk this part of your journey with you.

COPING WITH SINGLENESS

To develop your intimacy with Christ, ask the Bridegroom to reveal His delight in you, His desire for you, His committed presence with you, and His deep understanding of your soul.

RESOURCES

- *Sex and the Soul of a Woman: The Reality of Love and Romance in the Age of Casual Sex*, by Paula Rinehart
- *Real Sex: The Naked Truth about Chastity*, by Lauren Winner

- *Revelations of a Single Woman: Loving the Life I Didn't Expect*, by Connally Gilliam
- *Choices: Finding God's Way in Dating, Sex, Singleness, and Marriage*, by Stacy and Paula Rinehart
- *Gift-Wrapped by God: Secret Answers to the Question "Why Wait?"* by Linda Dillow and Lorraine Pintus

SEXUAL ABUSE, ASSAULT, RAPE, PROMISCUITY, AND SEXUALLY TRANSMITTED DISEASES

Sexual abuse is rampant in our culture and around the world. So are sexually transmitted diseases. If you have experienced sexual abuse or are at risk for a sexually transmitted disease, please seek a support group and/or professional help.

Schizophrenic is the best way to describe modern society's view of sexuality. . . . Society's schizophrenia develops from an attempt to reduce sex between humans to a purely physical . . . Yet any rape counselor knows that the real violence occurs on the inside and may lead to years of depression, nightmares, memory loss, and sexual dysfunction. Victims of abusive relatives and pedophiliac priests testify that something far more than a body gets hurt when a trusted adult abuses a child sexually. Decades later suffering persists.

— PHILIP YANCEY, *RUMORS OF ANOTHER WORLD*

RESOURCES

- *Sexual Assault: Will I Ever Feel Okay Again?* by Kay Scott
- *The Wounded Heart: Hope for Adult Victims of Childhood Sexual Abuse*, by Dr. Dan B. Allender
- *Gift-Wrapped by God: Secret Answers to the Question "Why Wait?"* by Linda Dillow and Lorraine Pintus
- *Sex and the Soul of a Woman: The Reality of Love and Romance in the Age of Casual Sex*, by Paula Rinehart
- *A Return to Modesty*, by Wendy Shalit
- *What Our Mothers Didn't Tell Us*, by Danielle Crittenden
- *No Stones: Women Redeemed from Sexual Shame*, by Marnie C. Ferree

ABORTION AND UNWANTED PREGNANCY

Few decisions are more heart-rending and emotionally scarring than the decision to end an unwanted pregnancy by getting an abortion. This is a complex issue, often involving a conflict of perceived rights. It also forces one to grapple with difficult questions such as, "When does life begin? When is the fetus really a person with a soul?" But for Christians, even deeper issues arise, such as the source of the sanctity of human life and the "rights" of the sovereign God over the life He creates (see **Genesis 9:6; Jeremiah 1:4-5; Psalm 139:13-**

16; and **Ezekiel 16**). The resources listed below can help you (or someone you know) either before or after an abortion.

Abortion is a global issue. The lives of tens of millions of babies are terminated each year. Couples and individuals faced with the challenge of an unwanted baby or a problem pregnancy deserve our compassion regardless of where they fall on the scale of political or biblical "correctness."

— PHILIP YANCEY, *RUMORS OF ANOTHER WORLD*

RESOURCES

- *Her Choice to Heal*, by Sydna Masse and Joan Phillips
- *A Season to Heal*, by Luci Freed and Penny Yvonne Salazar
- *Fatherhood Aborted*, by Guy Condon and David Hazard. Ministering to fathers whose children have been aborted.
- *No Stones: Women Redeemed from Sexual Shame*, by Marnie C. Ferree
- *Abortion: A Rational Look at an Emotional Issue*, by R. C. Sproul. Especially good for exploring the theological and biblical issues surrounding abortion.

PORNOGRAPHY, MASTURBATION, CYBERSEX, AND SEXUAL ADDICTIONS

So you look at porn, and sometimes masturbate. What's the big deal? Everybody does it. And besides, how can you avoid it these days? In response to these questions and excuses, research shows that porn is both destructive and highly addictive. The Bible says that it is practically adultery — like having "an affair of the mind." If you've ever gotten hooked and tried to free yourself, then you know how porn and other sexual practices can put you in bondage. Believe that hope and freedom are possible! These resources can help.

Pornography revenue in the U.S. is higher than the combined revenues of all professional football, baseball, and basketball franchises, ranking $12-14 billion annually.

— FROM "HAS AMERICA BECOME A PORN NATION?" BY ELIZABETH CAMERON,
CAMPUS CRUSADE TODAY, APRIL, 2007.

RESOURCES

- *Breaking Free: Understanding Sexual Addiction & the Healing Power of Jesus*, by Russell Willingham
- *False Intimacy: Understanding the Struggle of Sexual Addiction*, by Dr. Harry W. Schaumburg
- *Falling Forward: The Pursuit of Sexual Purity*, by Craig Lockwood
- *An Affair of the Mind*, by Laurie Hall

- *The Struggle*, by Steve Gerali
- *Contrary to Love: Healing the Sexual Addict*, by Patrick Carnes
- *Recovering from Infidelity and Overcoming Sexual Addiction*, audio by H. B. London, Focus on the Family
- *Every Man's Battle*, by Steven Arterburn
- *Every Young Man's Battle*, by Steven Arterburn
- *Every Young Woman's Battle*, by Steven Arterburn and Shannon Ethridge

ORGANIZATIONAL RESOURCES:

- National Association for Christian Recovery (http://www.christianrecovery.com). This organization provides information on Christian 12-step recovery groups and related resources.
- Covenant Eyes (http://www.covenanteyes.com). This organization assists those struggling with Internet pornography by offering a great filter and also helping with accountability, among other services.
- New Life Ministries (www.newlifeministries.com). This ministry provides counseling resources and workshops for men involved in sexual sin or temptation and workshops for women in relationships with men involved in pornography or adultery.
- For married women whose husbands are involved in or recovering from pornography or infidelity: www.everyheartrestored.com. For men who are looking for God's wisdom in keeping themselves sexually pure: www.everymansbattle.com.

GENDER IDENTITY AND CONFUSION

The bell curve of sexual behavior has been expanded to include homosexuality, bisexuality, bestiality, transsexuality, and androgyny (blending male and female), alongside the biblical ideals of virginity and monogamous, lifetime heterosexual marriage relationships. The popular media raise our awareness of these options as never before. No wonder some of us are confused about gender issues. For some people, confusion about gender may also have roots in unresolved issues from childhood. Again, the Bible offers hope in this area.

RESOURCES

- *Falling Forward: The Pursuit of Sexual Purity*, by Craig Lockwood
- *Strength in Weakness: Healing Sexual and Relational Brokenness*, by Andrew Comiskey
- *A Parent's Guide to Preventing Homosexuality*, by Joseph Nicolosi and Linda Ames Nicolosi
- *Crisis in Masculinity*, by Leanne Payne

HOMOSEXUALITY

Traditionally, even talking about homosexuality has been taboo in some Christian circles. However, in today's world this issue has come out of the closet and impacts societies, families, politics, and the church, to name only a few. Biblical passages from both the Old and New Testament speak against practicing homosexuality. See **Genesis 19:1-7; Leviticus 18:22; Romans 1:26-27; Ephesians 2:1-5**. It is no secret that people are divided about homosexuality. In this study we can't possibly deal with all the voices speaking for and against homosexuality. We encourage you to examine the Bible on the topic and to extend love in Jesus' name to all people.

RESOURCES

- *Strength in Weakness: Healing Sexual and Relational Brokenness*, by Andrew Comiskey
- *When Homosexuality Hits Home: What to Do When a Loved One Says They're Gay*, by Joe Dallas
- *"The Crisis of Homosexuality,"* a *Christianity Today* series edited by J. Isamu Yamamoto
- *Setting Love in Order: Hope and Healing for the Homosexual*, by Mario Bergner
- *Crisis in Masculinity*, by Leanne Payne
- *Healing Homosexuality*, by Leanne Payne
- *Homosexuality and the Politics of Truth*, by Jeffrey Satinover, M.D.
- *Pursuing Sexual Wholeness*, by Andrew Comiskey
- *Someone I Love Is Gay: How Family and Friends Can Respond*, by Anita Worthen and Bob Davies

ORGANIZATIONAL RESOURCES

- Exodus (www.exodusglobalalliance.org) acts as the umbrella organization for many evangelical ex-gay ministries. Their mission is "Proclaiming that change is possible for the homosexual through the transforming power of Jesus Christ." They equip Christians and churches to uphold the biblical view of sexuality, and also respond with compassion and grace to those affected by homosexuality.
- Pure Intimacy (www.pureintimacy.org) is a ministry associated with Focus on the Family that addresses intimacy and addiction, homosexuality, and a theology of sexuality.
- Desert Stream (www.desertstream.org) aims to minister the life of Jesus to the relationally and sexually broken.

INFERTILITY, CHILDLESSNESS, AND MISCARRIAGE

These can become painful issues for many reasons: medical problems, sexually transmitted diseases (STDs), the death of a child, or singleness, for starters. More often these days, both married and single people are adopting children to address the loneliness related to infertility and childlessness. But often these conditions impact negatively our sense of masculinity or femininity, causing some to feel incomplete or ashamed. And that can lead to damage in marriage relationships and, ultimately, to deep disappointment with God. If you struggle with any of these, why not find a support group or seek out the help of a professional?

RESOURCES

- *Hannah's Hope: Seeking God's Heart in the Midst of Infertility*, by Jennifer Saake
- *Water from the Rock: Finding God's Comfort in the Midst of Infertility*, by Becky Garrett, Donna Gibbs, and Phyllis Rabon
- *Miscarriage: Women Sharing from the Heart*, by Marie Allen and Shelly Marks
- *A Hope Deferred: A Couple's Guide to Coping with Infertility*, by Jill Baughan
- Mommies Enduring Neonatal Death (http://www.mend.org) serves mothers who have suffered a miscarriage.

INFIDELITY, MARITAL LIFE, AND PROBLEMS

Getting married is easy. But enjoying romance, intimacy, friendship, and satisfaction across one's lifespan in marriage is challenging. If you are struggling in marriage, these resources can help.

RESOURCES

- Read the Song of Solomon for ideas on romance.
- *The Mystery of Marriage: As Iron Sharpens Iron*, by Mike Mason
- *Solomon on Sex*, by Joseph C. Dillow
- *Intended for Pleasure*, by Ed and Gaye Wheat
- *Rebuilding Your Broken World*, by Gordon MacDonald
- *Restoring the Fallen*, by Sandy Wilson, Paul Friesen, Virginia Friesen, and Larry Paulson
- *Torn Asunder: Recovering from Extramarital Affairs*, by Dave Carder (book and workbook)
- *Recovering from Infidelity and Overcoming Sexual Addictions* (two cassette tapes), by H. B. London, Focus on the Family
- *Every Heart Restored* (and Workbook), by Stephen Arterburn, Fred Stoeker, and Mike Yorkey

ORGANIZATIONAL RESOURCES

- Family Life (www.familylife.com) is a division of Campus Crusade for Christ that provides practical, biblical tools to strengthen marriage and family relationships.
- American Association of Christian Counseling (AACC) (http://www.aacc.net) is a national Christian organization of professional counselors. The website provides a referral network of its membership.

A CLOJING WORD OF COMFORT

Apart from the presence of God, there is no deep healing for our grief. Time can make it easier, but that is all. The good news when our hearts are broken is that God invites us to freely mourn in the great space of His loving presence. Our pain does not threaten Him; it does not cause Him to fear that we will ruin His reputation. He is not repulsed with the ugliness we feel. Even when we hurt so much that we can hardly bear it, we are still His beloved.

— SALLY BREEDLOVE, *CHOOSING REST*

CHAPTER 6
SEXUALITY: HOW CAN I LIVE IT WELL?

When William married Kristie, he thought his sexual struggles would be over. She was beautiful and sexy and sweet — the woman of his dreams. During their engagement they had even managed to stay within the sexual boundaries, and he felt good about that. But now, four years into their marriage, he is spending way too much time on the Internet looking at pornography. Okay, so they aren't the really hard-core sites. But William realizes how crushed Kristie will be if she ever finds out. He is ashamed that he just can't seem to stay away, and he's afraid of losing her trust if she discovers what he is really doing late at night.

Something tells William that he should confide in Dan, his Bible study leader, about his struggles. But he doesn't want to risk losing Dan's respect. Besides, he isn't quite ready for the kind of man-to-man accountability that Dan will probably suggest. Maybe he isn't as serious about living well sexually as he likes to think he is.

In a culture without boundaries, acceptable talk about sexual limits often focuses on issues of health and safety. And issues of health and safety are reduced to discussions about condoms and birth control. But what about the health and safety of a [person's] heart and soul? Aren't they worth paying attention to?

— CONNALLY GILLIAM, *REVELATIONS OF A SINGLE WOMAN: LOVING THE LIFE I DIDN'T EXPECT*

PAUSE 1_EXPLORING WHAT GOD SAYS

There is a growing cry, not necessarily for a return to the nostalgic past, but for some new form of boundaries that protect the sacredness of sex. Especially for [people] who long ago lost their virginity, there is a longing to regain the innocence of soul that boundaries imply. . . . Many of us give away something precious before we know what we have. No one in our lives alerts us to our vulnerability; no one values our sexuality enough to struggle for its protection. Or perhaps we do not allow ourselves to hear One who wants to help.

— PAULA RINEHART, *SEX AND THE SOUL OF A WOMAN*

Living well in any area of life involves understanding and setting boundaries. Consider these words of David:

> PSALM 16:5-6. LORD, *you have assigned me my portion and my cup; you have made my lot secure. The boundary lines have fallen for me in pleasant places; surely I have a delightful inheritance.*

The boundaries here were geographical, referring to the territory God bestowed on His people in the Promised Land. If we make a parallel here, what other boundaries relating to one's body or life (besides sexual ones) does a wise person stay within in order to live life well?

Why would anyone choose to live within boundaries?

What is your attitude toward having sexual boundaries?

Here are just a few of the many passages about sex in the Bible. We've selected these because they express God's best for us — the "grace boundaries" that come from God's protectively jealous love for us. These boundaries are both a gift of His grace and a part of His design.

In the margin next to each passage, try to summarize the core idea(s) from the passage in a short phrase or sentence.

What we do with our bodies, what we do sexually, shapes our persons. How we comport ourselves sexually shapes who we are.

— LAUREN WINNER, *REAL SEX: THE NAKED TRUTH ABOUT CHASTITY*

HONORING SEXUALITY

CORE IDEA(S)

1 TIMOTHY 5:1-2. Do not rebuke an older man harshly, but exhort him as if he were your father. Treat younger men as brothers, older women as mothers, and younger women as sisters, with absolute purity.

Is absolute purity even possible? What do you think purity would look like in your relationships with others?

The Bible (especially the Song of Solomon) celebrates the power of feminine and masculine beauty. So how can you honor beautiful and powerful sexuality in other people without crossing the threshold of lust?

How do you think singles can express their sexuality "with absolute purity"? (1 Timothy 5:2)

How do you think married people can express their sexuality "with absolute purity"? (1 Timothy 5:2)

SEXUALITY AND SINGLENESS

To be premaritally chaste is not to sit passively by and simply avoid sex; it is to participate in an active protection of a created good. . . . And premarital sex itself — even premarital sex between two people who love each other — forms in us false sexual habits, habits that ultimately do violence to marital sex. . . . The unmarried Christian who practices chastity refrains from sex in order to remember that God desires your person, your body, more than any man or woman ever will.

— *LAUREN WINNER, REAL SEX: THE NAKED TRUTH ABOUT CHASTITY*

CORE IDEA(S)

1 CORINTHIANS 7:32-38. I want you to be free from the concerns of this life. An unmarried man can spend his time doing the Lord's work and thinking how to please him. But a married man has to think about his earthly responsibilities and how to please his wife. His interests are divided. In the same way, a woman who is no longer married or has never been married can be devoted to the Lord and holy in body and in spirit. But a married woman has to think about her earthly responsibilities and how to please her husband.

35 I am saying this for your benefit, not to place restrictions on you. I want you to do whatever will help you serve the Lord best, with as few distractions as possible.

36 But if a man thinks that he's treating his fiancée improperly and will inevitably give in to his passion, let him marry her as he wishes. It is not a sin. But if he has decided firmly not to marry and there is no urgency and he can control his passion, he does well not to marry. So the person who marries his fiancée does well, and the person who doesn't marry does even better. (NLT)

The apostle Paul never married, as far as we can tell from the Bible. Neither did Jesus or Daniel, to name some other famous biblical singles. How do you think their singleness affected their contribution to God's Kingdom?

What about being single do or did you enjoy most? What about being single do or did you enjoy least?

In a few words, describe how each of these realities affects you as a sexual being:

• Living in a highly sexualized culture

• The loneliness of singleness

• Jealousy

How do these factors influence your walk with God?

SEX WITHIN MARRIAGE

Our task is not to cultivate moments when eros can whisk us away from our ordinary routines, but rather to love each other as eros becomes imbedded in, and transformed by, the daily warp and woof of married life. For in household sexuality, we see the ways our daily human struggles offer the only language we have to call ourselves to God's grace.

— LAUREN WINNER, *REAL SEX: THE NAKED TRUTH ABOUT CHASTITY*

CORE IDEA(S)

GENESIS 2:24. For this reason a man will leave his father and mother and be united to his wife, and they will become one flesh.

SONG OF SOLOMON 5:8-16

SONG OF SOLOMON 7:1-6

How do these passages encourage you — or discourage you — about the beauty of sex in marriage?

Notice what "grace boundaries" the Bible draws for sex in these verses. Also notice what consequences occur when we violate those boundaries.

PROVERBS 5:15-18. Drink water from your own well — share your love only with your wife. Why spill the water of your springs in the streets, having sex with just anyone? You should reserve it for yourselves. Never share it with strangers. Let your wife be a fountain of blessing for you. Rejoice in the wife of your youth. (NLT)

1 CORINTHIANS 7:3-5. The husband should fulfill his marital duty to his wife, and likewise the wife to her husband. The wife's body does not belong to her alone but also to her husband. In the same way, the husband's body does not belong to him alone but also to his wife. Do not deprive each other except by mutual consent and for a time, so that you may devote yourselves to prayer. Then come together again so that Satan will not tempt you because of your lack of self-control.

HEBREWS 13:4. Marriage should be honored by all, and the marriage bed kept pure, for God will judge the adulterer and all the sexually immoral.

What do you think the Bible means when it says that a person's body belongs to the spouse alone? Why do you think this mutual possessiveness is important in a marriage?

LIMIT/ ON /EXUAL PARTNER/

In the margin, identify any sexual partners that God puts "out of bounds" for His children. Also underline any negative consequences or reasons given for these boundaries.

FORBIDDEN SEXUAL PARTNERS
AND CONSEQUENCES

Animals (bestiality) ⟶ death

EXODUS 22:19. Anyone who has sexual relations with an <u>animal</u> must be put to <u>death</u>.

EXODUS 20:14. You shall not commit adultery.

LEVITICUS 18:6-16. (read from your Bible)

MATTHEW 5:27-28. You have heard that it was said, "Do not commit adultery." But I tell you that anyone who looks at a woman lustfully has already committed adultery with her in his heart.

1 CORINTHIANS 6:13-20. "Food for the stomach and the stomach for food" — but God will destroy them both. The body is not meant for sexual immorality, but for the Lord, and the Lord for the body. By his power God raised the Lord from the dead, and he will raise us also. Do you not know that your bodies are members of Christ himself? Shall I then take the members of Christ and unite them with a prostitute? Never! Do you not know that he who unites himself with a prostitute is one with her in body? For it is said, "The two will become one flesh." But he who unites himself with the Lord is one with him in spirit.

ROMANS 1:26-27. Because of this, God gave them over to shameful lusts. Even their women exchanged natural relations for unnatural ones. In the same way the men also abandoned natural relations with women and were inflamed with lust for one another. Men committed indecent acts with other men, and received in themselves the due penalty for their perversion.

According to these verses, what's wrong with having sex with partners other than our marriage partner?

Since Christ lives in the hearts of believers, how do you think He responds and feels when a believer engages in or fantasizes about sexual immorality?

PROTECTNG THE SACREDNESS OF SEX

QUICK BACKGROUND: Joseph was a man with a God-given dream that he would have significant influence with others, including his brothers, who would bow down to him one day. God's process of exalting Joseph began by first humbling him over many years through experiences of violence, imprisonments, and other difficulties. In the passage below, when Joseph was serving as an overseer in the house of an Egyptian officer, he was powerfully enticed by the officer's wife.

Read Joseph's story from GENESIS 39:6-18. Identify and describe any attitudes, convictions, or actions that helped Joseph respond well to sexual temptation and remain sexually pure during this period of vulnerability.

If Joseph had yielded to this sexual temptation, what effect do you think it would've had on his destiny?

Have you been trying to deal with sexual struggles and temptations alone? How successful has that strategy been for you?

PROVERBS 7:6-21 describes what happens to a young man who falls for a seductive woman. From this passage, what would you say are two or three lessons God wants us to learn?

The Bible urges us both to "resist the devil" (James 4:7) and to "flee youthful lusts" (2 Timothy 2:22) when facing temptation. How does Joseph's story illustrate both ways of successfully protecting the sacredness of sexuality?

From what you've studied so far, what motivates you to live well sexually?

PAUSE 2_EXPLORING YOUR REALITY

Some great and powerful men and women have suc-
cumbed to the power of sexual temptation. Name a few
public figures whose sexual misbehaviors made the
headlines. What consequences have come from their
choices?

In your youth, who were your role models for sexual behavior? Compare those role models
with the guidelines for sexual behavior you just studied. How do they stack up?

Consider the TV shows or movies you've watched recently. How has the media view of
sexuality affected your thoughts and desires about living as a sexual being?

In GENESIS 2:18 God said it wasn't good for man to be alone, so He created Eve. How does
each of these emotional factors impact your sexual desires and choices:

• Being lonely

• Being alone

• Your desire to be known

These days, seductive men and women are just a mouse click away because of the Internet. What does pornography do to your soul?

How can you protect yourself from pornography and its negative impact?

Sometimes we develop an elaborate "back-room life" where we give in to our sexual lust. Where have you been giving yourself permission to go that you need to put off limit?

In going there, what do you think you've been running *from*?

In staying within boundaries, what do you think you might be running *to*?

[Believers] who remain in hiding continue to live the lie. We deny the reality of our sin. In a futile attempt to erase our past, we deprive the community of our healing gift. If we conceal our wounds, out of fear or shame, our inner darkness can neither be illuminated nor become a light for others. But when we dare to live as forgiven men and women, we join the wounded healers and draw closer to Jesus.

— BRENNAN MANNING, *THE RABBI'S HEARTBEAT*

PAUSE 3_COMING ALIVE TO GOD AND OTHERS

The Bible provides practical suggestions to deal with sexual temptation. For each passage below, express the main idea(s) or the advice in the verse. Then describe specifically when and how you might apply this key in your own life.

VERSE	KEY THOUGHT	APPLICATION
JOB 31:1. I made a covenant with my eyes not to look with lust at a young woman. (NLT)	I can't help the first look, but I can refuse to take the second look.	I will install a good filter on my computer to keep out the porn—and do it today!
ECCLESIASTES 4:9-10. Two people are better off than one, for they can help each other succeed. If one person falls, the other can reach out and help. But someone who falls alone is in real trouble. (NLT)		
ROMANS 6:12-13. Therefore do not let sin reign in your mortal body so that you obey its evil desires. Do not offer the parts of your body to sin, as instruments of wickedness, but rather offer yourselves to God, as those who have been brought from death to life; and offer the parts of your body to him as instruments of righteousness.		
2 TIMOTHY 2:22. Run from anything that stimulates youthful lusts. Instead, pursue righteous living, faithfulness, love, and peace. Enjoy the companionship of those who call on the Lord with pure hearts. (NLT)		

VERSE	KEY THOUGHT	APPLICATION
HEBREWS 3:13. Help each other to stand firm in the faith every day, while it is still called "today," and beware that none of you becomes deaf and blind to God through the delusive glamour of sin. (PH)		
1 JOHN 1:7-9. But if we are living in the light, as God is in the light, then we have fellowship with each other, and the blood of Jesus, his Son, cleanses us from all sin. If we claim we have no sin, we are only fooling ourselves and not living in the truth. But if we confess our sins to him, he is faithful and just to forgive us our sins and to cleanse us from all wickedness. (NLT)		
JAMES 5:16. Confess your sins to each other and pray for each other so that you may be healed. The earnest prayer of a righteous person has great power and produces wonderful results. (NLT)		

CLOSING THOUGHTS

Most of us tend to keep our sexual tensions and struggles trapped inside us — in darkness. We can start feeling incredibly ashamed that we even have struggles. But still more terrifying can be the possibility of facing condemnation by others if our struggles are exposed for what they really are. So we hide, like Adam and Eve. Creating environments of safety based on grace and truth will allow others to come into God's healing light.

Left unresolved, these issues can eat away at us or end up cutting us off from the very things that are meant to give us life. But if we will risk taking these things — the very things we fear could ruin us if they are found out — and bring them into the light of God's truth, we begin to see our temptations as shabby substitutes for the real thing. When we humble ourselves in confession to God and to appropriate grace-based people about the reality of our sinfulness and struggles, we will find hope and grace and freedom for the journey.

PRAYER PAUSE

Take some time to pray over anything God has impressed on you during this study.

PAUSE 4_JOURNEYING FORWARD

ACTS 22:8,10.   Who are you, Lord?
                    What shall I do, Lord?

How have you experienced God this week?

Select one verse or passage from this chapter that was meaningful to you this week, and write it here.

We live in a world of images that deeply influence how we look at life. Choose a picture from this chapter that is meaningful or disturbing to you, and briefly explain why.

Reflecting on what was most meaningful to you from this chapter, respond to one (or more) of these questions in the journal on the next page:

- Who are you, Lord? (an insight into God's character or heart)
- What shall I do, Lord? (an idea for practical application)
- Who shall I be, Lord? (a sense of personal identity)
- Other response?

JOURNAL

CHAPTER 7
EMOTIONS: FRIENDS OR FOES?

He cheated on her. He was the husband and father that everyone pointed to, and every wife screamed, "Why can't you be more like him?" when she wanted to make her husband jealous. He was the businessman that everyone respected for his blameless integrity. He was the pillar in the church that other men asked advice from. He was my dad.

And God watched in silence. I remember because I tried to listen, but I couldn't hear anything beyond her crying. Her disturbing wails penetrated my heart in the innocence of her pain. She sat against the wall, trembling in fear and anger and pain. He sat on the bed, pleading for forgiveness but wanting her to hate him. I sat in my room, not understanding. . . .

Pain touched my soul. It shattered my dreams and my relationships and my faith in only a moment. It dropped my life like a mirror on a rock. And then I wanted to feel and not move, to allow my pain to consume me or to be consumed by the struggle of why. But . . . I required the pain of a moment to realize the aching of my entire life. . . .

I am grateful for the pain. Like a mother trembles as she breaks her own body to give life, a heart has to shatter for a soul to burst forth, gasping for air. My willingness to trust has become a choice. Love and faith and hope are no longer ideas but braces holding the pieces of my brokenness in a new beauty. I watch my family sitting. She is healing. He is learning. My brother is hurting. I am hoping. God is redeeming.[1] — Adam Schaechterle

Can you relate to Adam's story? Or does this remind you of anyone? Explain.

---

[1] By Adam Schaechterle. © 2006 Relevant Media Group. Excerpted from "The Answer to Why," *RELEVANT* magazine.com, April 20, 2005. Used with permission. Read Adam's whole story on the website. Used by permission.

PAUSE 1_EXPLORING WHAT GOD SAYS

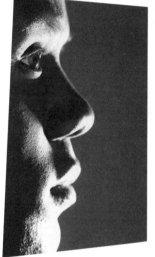

The CONNECT series is about experiencing deep inner change. As we experience transformation in our sexual identity, it influences our emotional world. God longs to bring transformational change to our emotional world, too.

Each of us has an "emotions menu" that we select from day by day. In the last twenty-four hours, which items on the "emotions menu" have you sampled? Do your tears indicate underlying fears or hopelessness — or even perhaps genuine joy? Does your road rage suggest that you need an anger management course? Or do you prefer to operate on numbness, showing an "I-don't-care" face to the world? Wherever you are at this moment on the emotional roadmap, this chapter will help you explore your emotional world.

Our emotions aren't the result of the Fall, either. Like other parts of our identity, we are emotional beings because we are created in the image of our emotion-ful God. Yes, God also feels emotions from His heart — including some we usually call "painful" emotions.

From these passages, what emotions do you see God has?

GOD HAS EMOTIONS

GOD'S EMOTIONS:

GENESIS 6:6. The Lord was grieved that he had made man on the earth, and his heart was filled with pain.

PSALM 18:19. He led me to a place of safety; he rescued me because he delights in me. (NLT)

ISAIAH 63:9. In all their distress he too was distressed, and the angel of his presence saved them. In his love and mercy he redeemed them; he lifted them up and carried them all the days of old.

HOSEA 11:8-9. How can I give you up, Ephraim? How can I hand you over, Israel? . . . My heart is changed within me; all my compassion is aroused. I will not carry out my fierce anger, nor will I turn and devastate Ephraim. For I am God, and not man — the Holy One among you. I will not come in wrath.

Add other verses you like . . .

THE UNUSUAL HEART OF GOD
God feels anger, fear, jealousy, despair, contempt . . . — and all of these emotions reveal something about his character. Most gloriously, each one points to the scandalous wonder of the Cross. . . . Our positive emotions, of course — joy, peace, pleasure, and others — have equal potential to teach us about the nature of God.

— DAN B. ALLENDER & TREMPER LONGMAN, *THE CRY OF THE SOUL*

How does it make you feel to realize that God has emotions?

The Bible does not mince words when describing the emotions of men and women. Instead, it recognizes the unexpected relationship between emotions and one's view of God. As you read the following stories, try to describe what each character in the story was probably feeling emotionally.

1 SAMUEL 20:27-34

SAUL:

OTHERS (Jonathan, David)

1 SAMUEL 1:1-18

HANNAH:

OTHERS (Elkanah, Peninnah, Eli)

When we have a goal that is blocked, or a desire that isn't being fulfilled, and none of our strategies are working, we often get emotional about it. What desires or goals did Saul and Hannah each have that were being blocked?

Saul refused to be humbly honest and vulnerable before God about his intense emotions. Hannah, on the other hand, seized the opportunity to pour out her hurting heart to God. How were the results different?

Of all the characters mentioned above, which one do you identify with at an emotional level? *Explain.*

From these verses, why should we both feel and express our feelings to God?

> PSALM 55:22. *Give your burdens to the LORD,*
> *and he will take care of you. He will not permit*
> *the godly to slip and fall.* (NLT)

> 1 PETER 5:7. *Cast all your anxiety on him because*
> *he cares for you.*

Describe one thing you struggle with — a burden or some kind of painful emotion — for which you most long to experience comfort, freedom, and release so you can move forward in your journey.

Imagine yourself describing this struggle in detail to God and asking for His help. What might that look like for you? What do you visualize Him doing with that issue?

Consider this verse. Why do you think the Bible invites us to confess our sins (and struggles) to others?

> JAMES 5:16. *Confess your sins to each other and pray for each other so that you may*
> *be healed. The earnest prayer of a righteous person has great power and produces*
> *wonderful results.* (NLT)

What could others provide for us that we need?

PAUSE 2_EXPLORING YOUR REALITY

In your opinion, are emotions negative or positive or neutral? What determines the difference?

Are you ever afraid of your own emotions? Other people's emotions? *Explain.*

Just as God's emotions flowed from His heart, so do ours. This means that our emotions can be an incredible mirror to help us be in touch with what's going on in the deep places of who we are.

Like the Titanic, boats can be shipwrecked by what is hidden under the water. Think of your life as an iceberg — where only 10 percent of it actually shows. Consider what emotions you personally might be keeping "below the water line." Take a minute to identify one emotional issue that you've kept hidden. Is there a better way to live in that emotion than you've been doing? *Explain.*

Consider this verse about the importance of paying attention to what's in our hearts:

> PROVERBS 4:23. *Guard your heart above all else, for it determines the course of your life.* (NLT)

From PROVERBS 4:23 and the quote by Curtis and Eldredge, what are some parts of your life that are affected by your heart?

What do you think it means to "guard your heart"? (NASB says, "Watch . . . with all diligence.")

What do you think it does *not* mean?

What do you think it would be like for you to live life without engaging your heart?

On the following scale mark where you usually find yourself in terms of your emotions.

Running from Emotions   Listening to Emotions   Wallowing in Emotions

Describe a time when you did one or more of these.

RUNNING FROM EMOTIONS	LISTENING TO EMOTIONS	WALLOWING IN EMOTIONS

What might we have to lose if we aren't emotionally authentic with God? . . . or if we aren't emotionally authentic with safe friends? *Explain.*

Emotions are the language of the soul. They are the cry that gives the heart a voice. To understand our deepest passions and convictions, we must learn to listen to the cry of the soul. However, we often turn a deaf ear — through emotional denial, distortion, or disengagement. We strain out anything disturbing in order to gain tenuous control of our inner world. We are frightened and ashamed of what leaks into our consciousness. In neglecting our intense emotions, we are false to ourselves and lose a wonderful opportunity to know God. We forget that change comes through brutal honesty and vulnerability before God.

— DAN B. ALLENDER AND TREMPER LONGMAN III, *THE CRY OF THE SOUL*

After considering these angles on emotions, and the quote above, do you view your emotions more as friends or as enemies? Why?

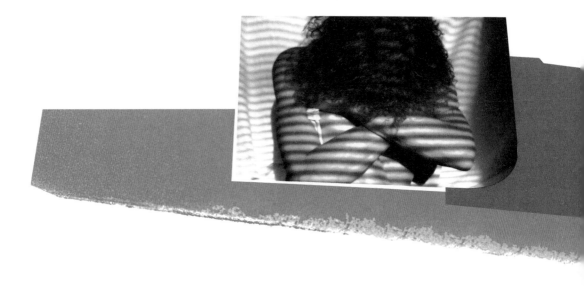

PAUSE 3_COMING ALIVE TO GOD AND OTHERS

God described David as "a man after his own heart" (1 Samuel 13:14). Read even a few of the many psalms that David wrote and you'll see how David was in touch with his emotions — from joy and praise to despair and anger. In his psalms, David shows us both how and why to be emotionally real with God. They reveal emotions as our friends, not our enemies . . . as a gift from God, not a curse . . . as something that thrusts us toward God rather than sending us into denial or hiding.

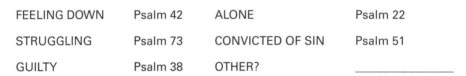

To help you come more alive to God about the emotional side of your being, devote as much time as you need to this activity.

1. SELECT one of David's psalms to meditate on and paraphrase. Choose any psalm that you connect with emotionally in the present. Or choose one of these:

FEELING DOWN	Psalm 42	ALONE	Psalm 22
STRUGGLING	Psalm 73	CONVICTED OF SIN	Psalm 51
GUILTY	Psalm 38	OTHER?	_____

2. READ it through several times, meditatively, in different versions, out loud, etc.
3. PROCESS it with your heart as much as with your mind.
4. Then REWRITE it on the following page, expressing it in your own words from your own heart.

YOUR PSALM

Wherever you are now on the journey of transformation in your heart, this is where the Holy Spirit is moving you. Meditate on God's promise to give His people new hearts.

> *EZEKIEL 11:19-20. I will give them an undivided heart and put a new spirit in them; I will remove from them their heart of stone and give them a heart of flesh. Then they will follow my decrees and be careful to keep my laws. They will be my people, and I will be their God.*

> *EZEKIEL 36:26-27. And I will give you a new heart, and I will put a new spirit in you. I will take out your stony, stubborn heart and give you a tender, responsive heart. And I will put my Spirit in you so that you will follow my decrees and be careful to obey my regulations.* (NLT)

What are the benefits and costs of living with a "heart of stone" or a "heart of flesh"?

What parts of your heart feel more like flesh, and what parts feel stony?

As Christ transforms your heart and life, how do you think this will impact you emotionally?

PRAYER PAUSE

As you reflect on this chapter, some might experience new areas of personal awareness, some may experience overwhelming emotions, and others may experience the pain of numb disconnectedness. Whatever you're experiencing, meditate on this verse for awhile. Invite Christ to speak to you about your emotional health and needs.

> *MATTHEW 11:28-30. Come to me, all you who are weary and burdened, and I will give you rest. Take my yoke upon you and learn from me, for I am gentle and humble in heart, and you will find rest for your souls. For my yoke is easy and my burden is light.*

PAUSE 4_JOURNEYING FORWARD

ACTS 22:8,10.   Who are you, Lord?
What shall I do, Lord?

How have you experienced God this week?

Select one verse or passage from this chapter that was meaningful to you this week, and write it here.

We live in a world of images that deeply influence how we look at life. Choose a picture from this chapter that is meaningful or disturbing to you, and briefly explain why.

Reflecting on what was most meaningful to you from this chapter, respond to one (or more) of these questions in the journal on the next page:

- Who are you, Lord? (an insight into God's character or heart)
- What shall I do, Lord? (an idea for practical application)
- Who shall I be, Lord? (a sense of personal identity)
- Other response?

JOURNAL

EMOTIONAL HEALTH — PROVERBS 4:23

Above all else, guard your heart, for it is the wellspring of life.

DIGGING DEEPER

Consider this description of an emotionally healthy heart. Then study the diagram below.

GALATIANS 5:22-23. But the fruit of the Spirit is love, joy, peace, patience, kindness, goodness, faithfulness, gentleness and self-control. Against such things there is no law.

An Authentic and Transforming Heart

What do you glean from this chart that helps you understand your emotional world?

PROCESSES THESE EMOTIONS:

	AND	
Numbness		Love
Shame		Joy
Grief		Goodness
Depression		Patience
False Happenings		Peace
Bitterness		Faithfulness
Anxiety		Self–Control
Fear		Gentleness
Anger		Kindness

EXPERIENCES THIS FRUIT:

In the midst of life's pain and pleasures

How does the fruit of the Spirit reflect not only character traits, but also an emotionally alive heart?

CHAPTER 8
MY EMOTIONAL WORLD: IS CHANGE POSSIBLE?

Latoya is at a point of disillusionment with her Christian faith. Since she met Christ three years ago, she has read her Bible and done many of the "Christian" behaviors — which she admits have been beneficial. But one issue just doesn't seem to be right. That issue is peace.

Jesus promised inner peace. Latoya's inner world seldom feels at peace. And every new relationship with a man stirs the pot of disillusionment.

As a child Latoya was sexually abused by an older cousin she had admired and trusted. Since then, her attempts to trust men — or to trust God, for that matter — have been disappointing.

No matter how much she seems to read the Bible and pray, her emotional world stays controlled by her past — not by any present sense of "the peace of God which transcends all understanding." She just can't seem to get beyond her unresolved questions, "Where was God when the abuse occurred? And why doesn't He bring His peace into this mess now?"

Latoya knows things have to change. If they don't, she'll simply walk away from her faith in disillusionment and go it on her own.

Can you identify with any of Latoya's issues — trust, unresolved hurt, disillusionment, lack of peace, etc.? If so, how might you empathize with Latoya?

Disillusionment like Latoya's happens to most of us sooner or later. Though the journey is different for each of us, some stops along the way are common. We start out being convinced. The ideas sound right . . . we can buy into the gospel with our heads because we really hope it's true . . . and we're glad it works for some people.

But somewhere along the line, our emotional world gets messed up . . . really messed up! Chaos. Havoc. We're afraid that all those promises of peace and contentment were . . . well, just illusions. That gospel we believed? It might still be powerful enough to heal others' issues. But our wounds go too deep. We just hurt too much to hang on to hope. Maybe we get angry that we were sold a bill of goods that isn't delivering what we expected. Or we just numb our hearts and put our deep feelings on mute to avoid facing the disappointment we feel toward God.

God's mysterious work of transforming us to be like Christ affects all parts of who we are — our identity and self-concept, our worldview and beliefs, our sexuality and behavior. Some of the deepest change happens when He begins to expose our emotional pain — and then begins the healing process. Sooner or later in life, all of us will need His radical heart surgery.

REALITY CHECK

People (especially men) are often uncomfortable even talking about "emotional struggles." Perhaps men can connect more easily with the idea of struggling with issues of some kind — bondage to pornography, bursts of anger, chronic frustration, compulsive workaholism, or some other dark feeling they can't shake. Others just feel emotionally numb or disconnected. Whatever the cause, there is often a sense of not experiencing the freedom Christ promised in a particular area.

Whatever your starting point, God desires to touch your heart at a deep level. Continue this journey with Him.

PAUSE 1_EXPLORING WHAT GOD SAYS

> Our dark emotions are much more than just uncomfortable feelings we struggle to control. They are windows into our heart. They are the cry of our soul. These emotions — the ones we tend to suppress and hide — actually have something important to tell us. They can reveal, in a very graphic way, where we are in our relationship with God. So often we find ourselves caught between extremes. Either we feel too much or not at all. We tend to ignore our feelings or fight them off as if they were an enemy. But all emotion — whether positive or negative — can give us a glimpse of the true nature of God. We want to control our negative emotions and dark desires. God wants us to recognize them as the cry of our soul to be made right with Him.
>
> — DAN B. ALLENDER & TREMPER LONGMAN, *THE CRY OF THE SOUL*

Disillusionment does not disqualify you as God's child. In fact, it is okay to go there, because God will meet you there, just as He has for others. Many of the great people of faith went through significant periods of emotional pain and disillusionment. As you look at these two stories, <u>notice how each man felt and why</u>. In the margin, note anything that strikes you about Jeremiah's emotional world.

HIS EMOTIONAL WORLD

JEREMIAH — THE WEEPING PROPHET

JEREMIAH 20:7-18. O Lord, you misled me, and I allowed myself to be misled. You are stronger than I am, and <u>you overpowered me</u>. Now <u>I am mocked</u> every day; everyone laughs at me. When I speak, the words burst out. "Violence and destruction!" I shout. So these messages from the Lord have made me a household joke. If I say I'll never mention the Lord or speak in his name, his word burns in my heart like a fire. It's like a fire in my bones! I am worn out trying to hold it in! I can't do it!

10 I have heard the many rumors about me. They call me "The Man Who Lives in Terror." They threaten, "If you say anything, we will report it." Even my old friends are watching me, waiting for a fatal slip. "He will trap himself," they say, "and then we will get our revenge on him." . . .

14 Yet I curse the day I was born! May no one celebrate the day of my birth. I curse the messenger who told my father, "Good news — you have

Felt overpowered by God

Being mocked; angry outbursts

a son!" Let him be destroyed like the cities of old that the Lord overthrew without mercy. Terrify him all day long with battle shouts because he did not kill me at birth. Oh, that I had died in my mother's womb, that her body had been my grave! Why was I ever born? My entire life has been filled with trouble, sorrow, and shame. (nlt)

Express what, if anything, from Jeremiah's emotional reality connects with you.

JEREMIAH'S COMFORT
AND CONFIDENCE

God would stand by him and fight for him.

JEREMIAH 20:11-13. <u>But the LORD stands beside me like a great warrior.</u> Before him my persecutors will stumble. They cannot defeat me. They will fail and be thoroughly humiliated. Their dishonor will never be forgotten. O LORD of Heaven's Armies, you test those who are righteous, and you examine the deepest thoughts and secrets. Let me see your vengeance against them, for I have committed my cause to you. Sing to the LORD! Praise the LORD! For though I was poor and needy, he rescued me from my oppressors. (NLT)

Where did Jeremiah find confidence and comfort in his emotional pain?

JOSEPH — THE MAN WITH THE WOUNDED HEART

Joseph was also a man with a wounded heart. Life had taught him much about abuse, betrayal, and bondage. He was an openly emotional man who cried often (mentioned at least seven times in his story). From the details of his story, he probably had good reasons for being disillusioned. (You can read about his early years in Genesis chapters 37 and 39.)

From the verses below, what <u>sins were committed</u> **against** Joseph in his early years that probably left deep wounds on his heart? What emotions did he probably feel about his family, himself, and God?

SCENE 1 (GENESIS 37:3-4,18-19,23-24,27-28)

SCENE 2

Fast-forward several decades to Joseph's mature years. Scripture suggests that Joseph experienced deep emotional healing, as described in this scene later in his life. Summarize in the margin <u>how Joseph found meaning and healing</u> from the emotional pain of his early years.

MEANING AND HEALING IN EMOTIONAL PAIN

GENESIS 50:14-21. After burying Jacob, Joseph returned to Egypt with his brothers and all who had accompanied him to his father's burial. But now that their father was dead, Joseph's brothers became fearful. "Now Joseph will show his anger and pay us back for all the wrong we did to him," they said. So they sent this message to Joseph: "Before your father died, he instructed us to say to you: 'Please forgive your brothers for the great wrong they did to you — for their sin in treating you so cruelly.' So we, the servants of the God of your father, beg you to forgive our sin." When Joseph received the message, he broke down and wept.

Then his brothers came and threw themselves down before Joseph. "Look, we are your slaves!" they said.

[19] But Joseph replied, "Don't be afraid of me. Am I God, that I can punish you? You intended to harm me, but God intended it all for good. He brought me to this position so I could save the lives of many people. [21] No, don't be afraid. I will continue to take care of you and your children." So he reassured them by speaking kindly to them. (NLT)

As you meditate on Joseph's life, try to express:

Any "lies" he might have come to believe about others, himself, or God:

The truth that set him free (Genesis 50:19-20):

The good that God accomplished through his pain, or what meaning he found:

The effects of his healing on his relationships with his brothers (Genesis 50:21):

Think over your life on these previous questions. Have you ever experienced someone harming you, and yet God accomplishing something good in the end? Explain.

PAUSE 2_EXPLORING YOUR REALITY

So much is distilled in our tears . . . not the least of which is wisdom in living life. I have learned that if you follow your tears, you will find your heart. And if you find your heart, you will find what is dear to God. And if you find what is dear to God, you will find the answer to how you should live your life.

— KEN GIRE, *WINDOWS OF THE SOUL*

Our present emotional world is shaped by our past. Some of us may need to look again at our past in order to see what God sees. In that way perhaps we can experience God's tender mercies in our present and be healed as we grow in intimacy with Him.

Much of our emotional world is formed by age twenty. As you reflect on your early years, how would you describe the emotional environment you grew up in?

Recall a pleasant memory from your childhood that still makes you smile. How do you respond emotionally to this memory?

Recall a painful memory from your childhood. What emotions are linked with this memory?

How do you deal with this memory and the emotions associated with it?

> *God usually doesn't heal what we refuse to feel.*
> — ANONYMOUS

2 CORINTHIANS 5:17 assures us that "if anyone is in Christ, he is a new creation; the old has gone, the new has come!" So you may tell yourself, "If the past is over and gone, then just let me forget it, and put it all behind me. Why should I talk about it? God forgives so I can forget about it. To what extent is this how you feel? *Explain.*

PRAYER PAUSE

Take time to worship and praise God for the good that has come from your childhood pleasure. Also pause for a while with God regarding your painful memory. Ask Him to meet you in this memory. How does He show up?

Check any of these emotions or issues that are still (or have been) significant in your experience:

____ discouraged	____ unfulfilled	____ hopeless
____ frustrated	____ betrayed	____ shameful past
____ confused	____ issues not resolved	____ fearful
____ nagging questions	____ problems not fixed	____ depressed
____ unmet expectations	____ things don't work out	____ other

Many young people today deal with their emotional pain by cutting themselves (or turning to other addictions). In your opinion, why do they do that? Do you think it helps?

If you found a friend of yours, or a brother or sister, numbing his or her heart with a dangerous behavior such as cutting, how would you offer them safety, comfort, and hope?

When we've been hurt emotionally or relationally, we often defend ourselves against further pain by vowing to "never" or "always" do something to protect ourselves, even if it is based on lies. Consider these common strategies for dealing with emotional pain. Can you identify with any of them?

1. PRONOUNCEMENTS = defining statements usually made over us by an authority figure that calls forth an identity, such as:
   - "You'll never amount to anything."
   - "You're so ugly, no man will ever want you."

Write any Pronouncements made about you.

2. LIES = false conclusions we come to because of difficult events or hurts, such as:
   - "All men are liars—you can't trust any of them."
   - "Marriage is for fools."

Write any Lies you came to believe.

3. VOWS = strong decisions we have made in order to avoid pain or to cope with it, such as:
   - "I will not feel emotion—it is too painful."
   - "I'll just have to take care of myself because nobody else will."
   - "I'll never be vulnerable again."

Write any Vows you made.

PRAYER PAUSE

Stop for five minutes or so. This is huge! Ask God to show you any pronouncements, lies, or vows you may be forgetting.

How does it make you feel to realize that lots of other people are walking the same road of disillusionment — and are meeting Jesus there?

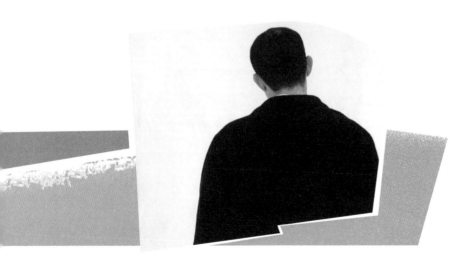

PAU/E 3_COMING ALIVE TO GOD AND OTHER/

Sometimes our painful emotions are the result of our own sinful choices, so we can't blame them on anyone else.

> *MARK 7:20-23. And then [Jesus] added, "It is what comes from inside that defiles you. For from within, out of a person's heart, come evil thoughts, sexual immorality, theft, murder, adultery, greed, wickedness, deceit, lustful desires, envy, slander, pride, and foolishness. All these vile things come from within; they are what defile you."* (NLT)

What emotions might spring from the work of sin within us?

Sometimes instead of changing, we just feel stuck in our emotional journey. If we have confessed all known sin, then perhaps there are emotional wounds that need to be healed. Consider your emotional struggles in light of Jesus' promise:

> *JOHN 8:32,36. Then you will experience for yourselves the truth, and the truth will free you. . . . So if the Son sets you free, you are free through and through.* (MSG)

What would it look like for you to be emotionally authentic with yourself? With others?

There's a huge difference between "knowing" about the ways of Jesus and "experiencing" life in Him. Before truth can set us free, we must trust that truth and experience it. Can you illustrate from your life something your head "knows" is true, but your heart is having a hard time trusting or "experiencing" it as being true for you?

EXAMPLE: I tell my friend at work that God can free him from his compulsion to drink. But secretly I don't believe God can heal my disappointment in my marriage.

EXAMPLE FROM YOUR LIFE:

As you read these passages, keep in mind whatever painful emotional "prisons" you have struggled with. From these verses, notice and mark how God longs to minister to our emotional needs and brokenness.

ISAIAH 61:1-3. The Spirit of the Sovereign LORD is upon me, for the LORD has anointed me to bring good news to the poor. He has sent me to comfort the brokenhearted and to proclaim that captives will be released and prisoners will be freed. He has sent me to tell those who mourn that the time of the LORD's favor has come, and with it, the day of God's anger against their enemies. To all who mourn in Israel, he will give a crown of beauty for ashes, a joyous blessing instead of mourning, festive praise instead of despair. In their righteousness, they will be like great oaks that the LORD has planted for his own glory. (NLT)

PSALM 147:3. He heals the brokenhearted and bandages their wounds. (NLT)

REVELATION 21:4. He will wipe every tear from their eyes. There will be no more death or mourning or crying or pain, for the old order of things has passed away.

From these verses, complete these statements in your own words:

GOD DESIRES US TO EXPERIENCE . . .

_____ for our broken hearts.

_____ from enslaving sin habits and limits due to our wounds.

_____ instead of emotional darkness (including despair).

_____ for those who mourn.

DIGGING DEEPER — PLEASE READ!

In most chapters of this study series, the Digging Deeper section is designed to be optional. This one is different. Before you leave this chapter, be sure to read through the helpful material in the Digging Deeper section. We strongly encourage you to set aside 1–2 hours for Listening Prayer — either alone or together with others. This time could be very significant in your spiritual journey toward wholeness in Christ.

REALITY CHECK

The scope of this series is limited. Some pains are so deep they may require gifted and skilled people to help you journey through the healing process. The discussion group you are in most likely is not prepared to help with traumatic memories. However, usually there are people in your area that can help you work through emotionally traumatic events. Please seek their help if needed.

TIME OF LISTENING PRAYER

Set aside some time to talk over your emotional struggles with God and to listen to Him speak into those issues and pain. Here are some simple guidelines to help you listen to God in prayer:

1. Still and quiet your soul. (Psalm 131:2)
2. Resist the enemy. (James 4:7)
3. Invite the Lord's presence.
4. Ask God to search your heart. (Psalm 139:23-24)
5. Ask God to speak to you. (1 Samuel 3:9-10)
6. Wait in silence. (Psalm 46:10; 62:5)
7. Write down and process whatever you hear God telling you during listening prayer.
8. Consider also processing with a trusted friend (James 5:16). Who is someone you could talk with and who would pray with you?

STEPS TO INNER HEALING THROUGH LISTENING PRAYER[1]

The Steps to inner healing are an attempt to help you listen to God over areas of repetitive emotional pain. However, emotional healing is rarely a step-by-step process — it is a living relationship and may not follow these steps. It is important to emphasize that it is up to God to answer these questions by revealing what's going on in your heart. It is not a matter of you having to figure out the answers and fix the problem.

STEPS TO INNER HEALING

STEPS	QUESTIONS TO ASK GOD
1. Identify the struggle or painful emotion God would have you deal with. Allow yourself to feel the emotion.	What repetitive negative emotion do You want me to focus on? Would You help me clarify or define this emotion? Is there a present situation causing me to feel this emotion now? Would You please help me to feel this painful emotion to provide a window into my soul?
2. Discovering the root wounding event.	When was the first time I experienced this emotion?
3. Discerning any lie that was believed.	In this painful event, what lie did I come to believe?
4. God reveals the truth.	What truth do You have to tell me about the lie I came to believe?
5. Experiencing His freedom.	Is there a second lie I came to believe in this painful event?
6. Discovering where Jesus was and/or what He was doing when the event took place.	Where were You, Jesus, when this happened to me? What were you doing and feeling back then?
7. Uncovering and renouncing any vows that may have been made.	Were there any vows I made during or after the wounding event to protect myself from future pain?
8. Extending and receiving forgiveness.	Am I willing to enter into the process of forgiving? Have I forgiven the long-term effects or consequences of the sin against me, as well as the act? Have I forgiven the one who hurt me? Have I forgiven myself? Have I come to peace with You for allowing the wounding event to take place? Did anyone make a pronouncement over me?

---

[1] Used by permission of the People Resources Team (PRT) of The Navigators.

STEPS	QUESTIONS TO ASK GOD
9. Identifying and breaking any pronouncements that may have been made over me.	Did the demonic world influence these painful events or my responses to them?
10. Identifying and breaking any demonic strongholds that may bind me.	Have demons been bound in Jesus' name and sent away? Has Your Holy Spirit healed these wounds?
11. Laying a persistent burden at the cross of Jesus.	Jesus, will You take this burden off me and carry it for me? What will You do with my burden?

PAUSE 4_JOURNEYING FORWARD

ACTS 22:8,10.   Who are you, Lord?
What shall I do, Lord?

How have you experienced God this week?

Select one verse or passage from this chapter that was meaningful to you this week, and write it here.

We live in a world of images that deeply influence how we look at life. Choose a picture from this chapter that is meaningful or disturbing to you, and briefly explain why.

Reflecting on what was most meaningful to you from this chapter, respond to one (or more) of these questions in the journal on the next page:

- Who are you, Lord? (an insight into God's character or heart)
- What shall I do, Lord? (an idea for practical application)
- Who shall I be, Lord? (a sense of personal identity)
- Other response?

JOURNAL

SUGGESTED MEMORY VERSE FOR THIS CHAPTER:

EMOTIONAL HEALING — PSALM 147:3

He heals the brokenhearted and bandages their wounds. (NLT)

CHAPTER 9
BEHOLDING GOD: HOW DOES HE TRANSFORM ME?

RAM'S STORY: *The journey of life was perplexing to Ram. One day, things seemed very clear, but the next day life was just emotional chaos. His relationships seemed to work at times; then at other times pain overwhelmed him. A while back a close friend had confronted him about his selfishness, greed, emotional detachment, and sometimes just plain rudeness. He knew he needed to change. Over the past year of walking with Jesus, he had seen some changes — even his friend had noticed. But now he wanted more change. The crush of life relationships, finances, and job demands simply didn't give him the time to really deal with his inner world. He had enough to do just holding things together.*

VICTORIA'S STORY: *To Victoria, life was exciting, an adventure in relationship. And things were going pretty smooth. Sure, there were bumps, but no cause for major rethinking of her plans. She fit in with others who had faith, but just didn't see the point of going deeper with God. "Live this life now, and go deep with God in the next world" was her perspective.*

Neither Ram nor Victoria felt much need to intentionally go deeper with God — at least for the present. What about you?

AN EXPERIENCE IN BEHOLDING

The word "behold" isn't used much any more — even though we do actually "behold" in our everyday lives. So to wrap our minds around what it means to "behold," enjoy this simple experience.

1. Take out a photograph of someone you love deeply.
2. Take a full five minutes to do nothing but gaze intently at this person's photograph. Turn off all distractions like the TV, music, cell phone, etc. During these five minutes, pay close attention not so much to what you're thinking, but more so to what you're feeling as you gaze into the face of this person who means so much to you. Okay, go for it!
3. (Five minutes later) Now journal your response to these questions.

JOURNAL

What is it you have been "seeing" with the eyes of your heart, and feeling in your heart as you "beheld" his or her face?

How is this experience of "beholding" a beloved face similar to what you might experience in worship?

PAUSE 1_EXPLORING WHAT GOD SAYS

The news about Jesus doesn't do us much good unless it invites us into a journey — a journey where we experience deep change at the level of our hearts and spirits, as well as in our behavior and relationships. The Bible calls this amazing and mysterious lifelong process "transformation." When transformation is happening, it means that God is changing us to become more and more like Jesus.

Spiritual transformation isn't something we do for God; it's something He does to us. But how does it happen? Is it the result of attending church, studying the Bible, or lots of prayer? Well, those may help. But at the core of God's transforming work in our lives is our growing passion to behold Him as He truly is.

BEHOLD = to look intently upon, gaze at, contemplate, and really comprehend what is seen.

So what is the connection between our beholding the triune God and His transforming us? To find out, let's really dig into the meaning of one important verse about spiritual transformation, using several different approaches.

Begin by meditating on this verse. Then answer a few basic what-who-how questions about its meaning.

2 CORINTHIANS 3:18. But we all, with unveiled face, beholding as in a mirror the glory of the Lord, are being transformed into the same image from glory to glory, just as from the Lord, the Spirit. (NASB)

What do we behold?

What is happening to us as we behold Him?

Who is doing the transforming, and for how long?

What everyday activity is compared to beholding God?

Anything else?

HISTORICAL BACKGROUND: The mention of an "unveiled face" in this verse can be confusing — unless you understand what it refers to in history. Check out the story (in Exodus 34:29-35) of Moses returning to the Israelite camp, carrying the stone tablets engraved with the Ten Commandments. Moses' face radiated the glory of God so much that the people could not look directly at him, and they were afraid. So he put on a veil to cover the glory, until it faded. In 2 Corinthians 3:12-17, Paul explains that an internal "veil" also covers the hearts of those who do not turn to the Lord. The veil is stripped off when a person comes to Jesus. Then we can begin to really see Him!

Here is 2 CORINTHIANS 3:18 again from several different Bible versions. As you meditate, sometimes just one word or small phrase may stand out to you. In the margin, summarize one new insight or shade of meaning that each version gives to you about beholding God and being transformed by God.

BEHOLDING GOD		BEING TRANSFORMED BY GOD
The more we look at Him, the more we reflect Him to others — like light bouncing off a mirror — and we are that mirror!	2 CORINTHIANS 3:18. So all of us who have had that veil removed can see and reflect the glory of the Lord. And the Lord—who is the Spirit—makes us more and more like him as we are changed into his glorious image. (NLT) 2 CORINTHIANS 3:18. But we Christians have no veil over our faces; we can be mirrors that brightly reflect the glory of the Lord. And as the Spirit of the Lord works within us, we become more and more like him. (TLB) 2 CORINTHIANS 3:18. And all of us, as with unveiled face, [because we] continued to behold [in the Word of God] as in a mirror the glory of the Lord, are constantly being transfigured into His very own image in ever increasing splendor and from one degree of glory to another; [for this comes] from the Lord [Who is] the Spirit. (AMP)	It happens gradually, as we become more and more like Jesus in character and heart.

It also helps to read the context of the key verse — meaning the verses that come before or after it. What additional insights do you notice about beholding God?

2 CORINTHIANS 3:16-18. Whenever, though, they turn to face God as Moses did, God removes the veil and there they are — face-to-face! They suddenly recognize that God is a living, personal presence, not a piece of chiseled stone. And when God is personally present, a living Spirit, that old, constricting legislation is recognized as obsolete. We're free of it! All of us! Nothing between us and God, our faces shining with the brightness of his face. And so we are transfigured much like the Messiah, our lives gradually becoming brighter and more beautiful as God enters our lives and we become like him. (MSG)

Beholding has to do with seeing God, personally present, alive and shining in all of His glory — at least as much as that is possible. How do you think beholding God and experiencing His presence helps to transform us into His image?

Now try paraphrasing 2 Corinthians 3:18 in your own words:

Do any new insights or questions strike you from these passages about beholding God and being transformed?

INSIGHTS ON BEHOLDING GOD AND
BEING TRANSFORMED

PSALM 37:4. Delight yourself in the LORD and he will give you the desires of your heart.

God says "Yes!" to my heart's desires. And He also plants new desires and dreams in my heart that come from Him!

PSALM 27:4. The one thing I ask of the L<small>ORD</small> — the thing I seek most — is to live in the house of the L<small>ORD</small> all the days of my life, delighting in the L<small>ORD</small>'s perfections and meditating in his Temple. (NLT)

DEUTERONOMY 5:24. You said, "Behold, the L<small>ORD</small> our God has shown us His glory and His greatness, and we have heard His voice from the midst of the fire; we have seen today that God speaks with man, yet he lives." (NASB)

ROMANS 8:29. God knew what he was doing from the very beginning. He decided from the outset to shape [to conform — NIV] the lives of those who love him along the same lines as the life of his Son. The Son stands first in the line of humanity he restored. We see the original and intended shape of our lives there in him. (MSG)

ROMANS 12:2. Do not conform any longer to the pattern of this world, but be transformed by the renewing of your mind. Then you will be able to test and approve what God's will is — his good, pleasing and perfect will.

ROMANS 12:2. Don't become so well-adjusted to your culture that you fit into it without even thinking. Instead, fix your attention on God. You'll be changed from the inside out. . . . God brings the best out of you, develops well-formed maturity in you. (MSG)

1 CORINTHIANS 13:12. Now we see but a poor reflection as in a mirror; then we shall see face to face. Now I know in part; then I shall know fully, even as I am fully known.

COLOSSIANS 3:1-4. Therefore if you have been raised up with Christ, keep seeking the things above, where Christ is, seated at the right hand of God. Set your mind on the things above, not on the things that are on earth. For you have died and your life is hidden with Christ in God. When Christ, who is our life, is revealed, then you also will be revealed with Him in glory. (NASB)

Now go back and put a star next to the best thing you discovered about beholding God and/or being transformed inwardly.

Consider how God chose to reveal Himself through the person of His Son Jesus.

> *HEBREWS 12:1-3. Therefore, since we have so great a cloud of witnesses surrounding us, let us also lay aside every encumbrance and the sin which so easily entangles us, and let us run with endurance the race that is set before us, fixing our eyes on Jesus, the author and perfecter of faith, who for the joy set before Him endured the cross, despising the shame, and has sat down at the right hand of the throne of God. For consider Him who has endured such hostility by sinners against Himself, so that you will not grow weary and lose heart.* (NASB)

What are several specific things that you know about God from observing the person and life of Jesus?

PAUSE 2_EXPLORING YOUR REALITY

For you, is "beholding God" . . .

____ seeing Him from a distance?

____ looking at Him, only to run away for fear of what you saw?

____ a glance at Him from time to time?

____ a regular gaze that is mutual and meaningful?

____ something else?

What traces of resistance or indifference are there in your heart to beholding God (if any)?

How might shame or guilt be contributing to feelings of resistance or indifference?

How do you think beholding God may help us worship Him?

Remember that beholding is a two-way process. God is beholding you, too. How do you respond to a God who beholds and delights in you 24/7?

Select one or two of the questions below to explore how you need or want to be transformed. Journal your responses below.

- How are the EMOTIONS of my heart being transformed in line with the fruit of the Spirit? (Galatians 5:22-23)
- How are my THOUGHTS and IMAGINATION being transformed?
- How is my WILL being transformed?
- How are the impulses and desires of my BODY being transformed?
- How am I embracing any of my new IDENTITIES in Christ (His disciple, bride, servant, etc.)?
- How is my SOUL being transformed into His image?
- Other?

JOURNAL

PAUSE 3_COMING ALIVE TO GOD AND OTHERS

God is everywhere — permeating every part of His creation and our existence. That means that we can behold Him everywhere, if we look for Him. From each verse, notice <u>what attribute of God is everywhere</u>. (Some passages have more than one answer.)

GOD'S _____ IS EVERYWHERE:

Glory, holiness

ISAIAH 6:3. Holy, holy, holy is the Lᴏʀᴅ Almighty; the whole earth is full of his glory.

ISAIAH 43:2. When you go through deep waters, I will be with you. When you go through rivers of difficulty, you will not drown. When you walk through the fire of oppression, you will not be burned up; the flames will not consume you. (ɴʟᴛ)

PSALM 19:1-4. The heavens proclaim the glory of God. The skies display his craftsmanship. Day after day they continue to speak; night after night they make him known. They speak without a sound or word; their voice is never heard. Yet their message has gone throughout the earth, and their words to all the world. (ɴʟᴛ)

PSALM 33:5. The Lᴏʀᴅ loves righteousness and justice; the earth is full of his unfailing love.

PSALM 139:7. I can never escape from your Spirit! I can never get away from your presence! (ɴʟᴛ)

ROMANS 1:20. For ever since the world was created, people have seen the earth and sky. Through everything God made, they can clearly see his invisible qualities — his eternal power and divine nature. So they have no excuse for not knowing God. (NLT)

In light of this verse and all you have learned, is following Jesus the best way of life to you? Are there other good options in your opinion?

JOHN 6:67-69. "You do not want to leave too, do you?" Jesus asked the Twelve. Simon Peter answered him, "Lord, to whom shall we go? You have the words of eternal life. We believe and know that you are the Holy One of God."

An old English hymn contains this line:

"When we see Him as He is, we'll praise Him as we ought."

Think about the effect it would have on our lives if we really could see God as He is — free from our cultural biases, spiritual blinders, hang-ups, and misconceptions. Deep inner change isn't some goal we pursue by sheer effort. True inner change is the blessed by-product of beholding God everywhere, always, throughout our life.

Finish these sentences some other ways:

When we see Him as He is, we'll _____ Him as we ought.

When we see Him as He is, we'll _____ Him as we ought.

Turn your eyes upon Jesus.
Look full in His wonderful face.
And the things of earth
will grow strangely dim
in the light of His glory and grace.

— "Turn Your Eyes Upon Jesus"
    (words and music by Helen Lemmel, public domain)

PRAYER PAUSE

Sometimes we want complete change now. Remember the freedom you've been given to talk to God about the expectations you put on yourself. Take time to enjoy His patience with you.

Imagine a lifestyle of beholding God. Pray through these verses and what they promise about the enjoyment of being close to God.

> PSALM 16:11. *You will make known to me the path of life; in Your presence is fullness of joy; in Your right hand there are pleasures forever.* (NASB)
>
> PSALM 25:14. *The secret [of the sweet, satisfying companionship] of the Lord have they who fear (revere and worship) Him, and He will show them His covenant and reveal to them its [deep, inner] meaning.* (AMP)

Consider what pleasures you tend to substitute for God's best pleasures. Also consider what it means for you to enjoy "The sweet, satisfying companionship" of God all the time. Continue in His presence for a while. . . .

Ask God to deeply reveal Himself to you. Also ask God to transform you as you behold Him. Ask Him to reveal areas of your life that need to be transformed into His glory. Sit with Him awhile. What is He saying to you?

PAUSE 4_JOURNEYING FORWARD

SOMEDAY . . . we will behold God face-to-face.

1 CORINTHIANS 13:12. For now we see in a mirror dimly, but then face to face; now I know in part, but then I will know fully just as I also have been fully known. (NASB)

1 JOHN 3:2. We know that when He appears, we will be like Him, because we will see Him just as He is. (NASB)

Someday, we will meet the great King and Author of history. Only then will our eyes be opened to the moments in which He was "the Lion" orchestrating events toward a greater purpose — a greater good. Only then will we better understand how and when the grand drama of providence intersected the smaller scenes of our lives.

— KURT BRUNER AND JIM WARE, *FINDING GOD IN THE LAND OF NARNIA*

When you see God face-to-face someday, what would you like Him to say to you?

What would you like to say to God?

What do you think you might understand then that you don't understand now?

JOURNAL

BEHOLDING GOD — 2 CORINTHIANS 3:18

And we, who with unveiled faces all reflect the Lord's glory, are being transformed into his likeness with ever-increasing glory, which comes from the Lord, who is the Spirit.

DIGGING DEEPER

The diagram [on page 170] offers one way to look at the big picture of our spiritual journey. From the beginning God created us in His own image and destined us to enjoy Him forever in heaven. But because of the Fall, we all go through a process of transformation and deep personal change as God develops Christ's character within us.

> 2 CORINTHIANS 3:18. And we, who with unveiled faces all reflect the Lord's glory, are being transformed into his likeness with ever-increasing glory, which comes from the Lord, who is the Spirit.

Consider the inner circle on the diagram. Which gifts of God's grace do you most connect with this week?

Consider the middle circle which reflects what we contribute to our own spiritual transformation. As you reflect on this study, what part does beholding God play in your spiritual transformation?

Last, consider the outer circle which describes how God's sovereign gifts and our contribution interact to produce deep personal change within us. Which aspect of the outer circle are you currently experiencing?

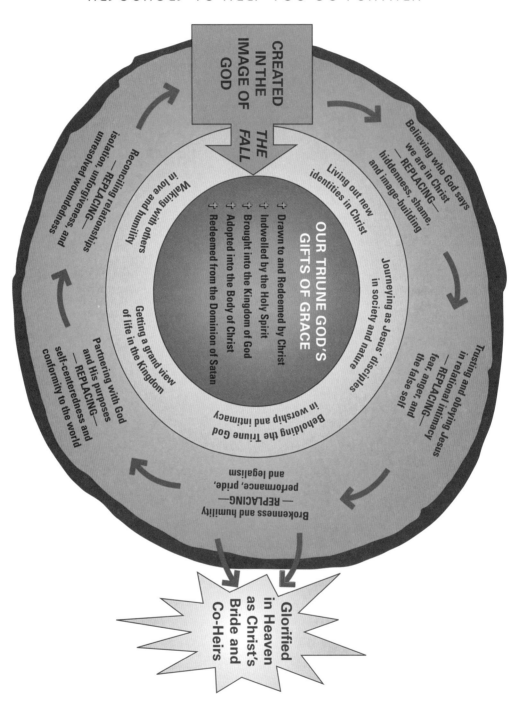

CREATED IN THE IMAGE OF GOD

THE FALL

Believing who God says we are in Christ — REPLACING — hiddenness, shame, and image-building

Living out new identities in Christ

Journeying as Jesus' disciples in society and nature

Trusting and obeying Jesus in relational intimacy — REPLACING — fear, anger, and the false self

Beholding the Triune God in worship and intimacy

Brokenness and humility — REPLACING — performance, pride, and legalism

OUR TRIUNE GOD'S GIFTS OF GRACE

✝ Drawn to and Redeemed by Christ
✝ Indwelled by the Holy Spirit
✝ Brought into the Kingdom of God
✝ Adopted into the Body of Christ
✝ Redeemed from the Dominion of Satan

Walking with others in love and humility

Reconciling relationships — REPLACING — isolation, unforgiveness, and unresolved woundedness

Getting a grand view of life in the Kingdom

Partnering with God and His purposes — REPLACING — self-centeredness and conformity to the world

Glorified in Heaven as Christ's Bride and Co-Heirs

170

CHAPTER 10
BEHOLDING GOD:
HOW DO I EXPERIENCE HIS PRESENCE?

This chapter is very different from the others, but the aim is the same: that we grow in intimacy with God. We'll suggest several "major highways" for you to consider on your spiritual journey — as well as several "scenic overlooks" to visit in order to behold God. Each of these creative processes can help you experience God more deeply. The idea is to begin developing a lifetime journey of deeply knowing the Triune God, Who is present everywhere, Who speaks through His living word, and Who jealously loves us.

Below is an overview of this chapter. Consider these as six broad "highways" to help you relate intimately with the Triune God through . . .

1. Beholding God Who Is Everywhere
2. Listening to God Who Speaks
3. Talking with God Who Listens
4. Honestly Examining Our Hearts Before Him
5. Presenting Ourselves to God
6. Building God's Kingdom with Him

Since there is no standard Bible study to prepare, how should you approach this chapter? Here's what we suggest:

1. This chapter contains a "menu" of many creative ways to behold God. No way are we suggesting that you try to do all of them. Begin by simply <u>reading through the chapter</u>.
2. As you read, <u>check or highlight</u> those that interest you the most.

3. Complete the chart at the end of the chapter on pages 179-180.
4. Then select one way of beholding God to try this week — not just once, but on several days this week. Most can be done alone, although a few also lend themselves to doing with someone else.
5. Make it an experimental journey that includes time to reflect on your experience. Choose an active way of recording or expressing your response, whether in writing or some other creative means.
6. Come to your small group meeting prepared to share your "beholding" experiences. Maybe read something from your journal. Also discuss with your group members how you might try beholding God together.
7. For the next week or two, select another approach to beholding God. Consider sampling something from each of the six "highways" over the next few months.
8. Expect to discover new things about the Lord along your journey.

1. BEHOLDING GOD WHO IS EVERYWHERE (PSALM 139:7-14)

VIEWING NATURE

- Walk or exercise in nature, and notice your surroundings. Ask God for a sense of awe and wonder. Ask God to speak to you through the natural things around you. How does beauty influence your time with God? Reflect on His presence everywhere — and beyond creation.

VISUAL ARTS REFLECTIONS

- After viewing a movie or TV program, ask yourself where God is in this movie? What would God consider to be emotionally honest about this movie? What would God consider to be good or evil in this movie?

SPIRITUAL SEXUALITY

- What does your sexuality tell you about being created in God's image? Ask God who He is jealous for. Are the jealousies of your heart aligned with the jealousies of God's heart?
- Christ is our bridegroom. Consider the ideal of marriage. Talk to Him about the marriages you see. Talk with Jesus about how you experience Him as your Bridegroom.
- Being alone without God — that is real loneliness. But being in Christ as a single is far from being alone. How does singleness shape your understanding of relating to God?

2. LISTENING TO GOD WHO SPEAKS (JOHN 1:1-14)

DRAMATIC READING OF THE SCRIPTURES

- After you read any story in Scripture, close your eyes and put yourself in the scene. How might those in this passage feel and think? What do you see, hear, smell, taste, and touch? Visualize the people in the scene. Where do you find yourself among them? What are you feeling? Doing? Saying? Journal your experiences.

FIVE SPIRITUAL TRANSFORMATION QUESTIONS (WHEN READING THE BIBLE)

- What does this passage say about how God views reality?
- What does this passage say about my intimacy with God?
- What does this passage say about the deep issues of my heart?
- What does this passage say about my relationship with others?
- What does this passage say about my relationship with nature?

MEMORIZING AND MEDITATING ON SCRIPTURE

- Select a favorite verse of Scripture to meditate on and memorize. Ask God to plant the truth of that verse deep in your heart — for life! Consider memorizing a paragraph or a longer passage. Read the surrounding verses, too, so that you can experience the flow of the context. Maybe put the verse to music.

LISTENING TO GODLY PEOPLE TEACH THE SCRIPTURES

- God has given the body of Christ gifted teachers who speak clearly of Jesus and His ways from personal experience. There are also those who neglect either the truth of Jesus or the ways of Jesus. Choose to listen to godly people who teach the Scriptures and practice the ways of Jesus. Read or listen to a message that has affected you.

SILENCE, SOLITUDE, AND LISTENING

- Sit silently for 10–30 minutes or more. Ask God to free your mind from the agendas and anxieties of life so that you can listen to Him. Mostly just enjoy being with the One who beholds you and says, "You're mine!" It brings Him great pleasure for you to sit quietly and stay focused on Him.

LISTENING TO MUSIC

- Listen to music that connects you with God. As you listen to the words and your heart resonates with the power of the music, ask God to minister to your soul as you praise Him aloud or in your heart.

SPENDING EXTENDED TIME WITH HIM

- Mark a day on your calendar for an extended time with God. Perhaps do this with others or by yourself. If with others, be with them in silence for the most part. Share what each of you has experienced at the end of your time.

3. TALKING WITH GOD WHO LISTENS (MATTHEW 6:5-14)

IN PRAYER

- Ask God to transform you in a particular way. For instance, pray that the depth of your intimacy with Him will grow beyond your wildest imagination over the next twelve months.
- A.C.T.S. (Adoration, Confession, Thanksgiving, and Supplication) is an acrostic that people use to help guide their time in prayer. Consider using A.C.T.S. or inventing an acrostic of your own that helps you walk through a worshipful time with God.
- Prayer Companions. Seeking God, simply to know Him better as opposed to asking Him for something, is a powerful way to experience Him with others. You are bringing two or more people's perspectives and experiences of God together and are therefore "multiplying the eyes" that are longing to get a look at God. It's an environment to receive from God and each other.
- Meditation. Meditate on a single characteristic of God, a word or phrase or thought that you heard or read — something that will focus you on a single point and shake your soul from distractions. If you find your mind wandering, it's okay. Just draw yourself back to that "one thing" again. Think of yourself as marinating in God's presence, soaking up the flavor of who He is.
- Retreat. Go exploring and find a special place where you can be with God in prayer. A private place helps free you to be honest with Him, express yourself to Him, and wrestle with Him. The Psalms were written by people who brought heart-rending, tough questions to God, along with their struggles. Consider reading the Psalms as a springboard for being real with God.

REMEMBERING / JOURNALING

- Keep a journal about your experience of God over a period of time. Make a life map to reflect on the joys and sorrows of your life and how God has met you on your journey.

CREATING

- Create poetry, a short story, a visual, or some music to express your spiritual journey.

REFLECTIVE HEALING

- Ask God to heal you. Remember wounds you have experienced in the past. Ask God to show you where He was in all that pain and how He desires to heal you (see chapter 7).

4. HONESTLY EXAMINING OUR HEARTS BEFORE HIM
(PROVERBS 4:23)

PULLING THE SPLINTER FROM MY OWN EYE (MATTHEW 7:3-5)

- Ask the Lord to reveal judgmental attitudes in your heart, where you've done the same thing that you've judged others for doing. Allow yourself to receive God's mercy. Ask Him for a merciful heart toward those you've judged.

CONFESSING AND REPENTING

- Ask God to reveal anything in your heart that is not pure. Ask for forgiveness and transformation. Receive His mercy and kindness.

MY AFFECTIONS, DESIRES, AND PASSIONS

- Think about your desires and affections — including sports, television and movies, video games, travel, causes, etc. Reflect on these questions: Where is God in this affection? How can I experience God in the midst of my other affections, desires, and passions?

FACING SHAME, GUILT, PAIN, PLEASURE, AND FINDING GOD'S MERCY AND JOY

- Shame, guilt, pain, and pleasure are all deep emotions that can lead us deeper into the heart of God. Ask God to reveal His way of mercy and joy as you experience these emotions.

SETTING OUR HOPES ON ETERNAL REALITIES

- Examine your God-given hopes and dreams. Where could they take you over the next 5–10 years? Consider inviting someone to speak into your dreams and spiritual journey.

LOVING GOD WITH ALL OUR HEARTS, MINDS, STRENGTH, AND SOULS

- God is the Lover of your soul. What aspects of your soul have not received His love? What aspects of your soul are not deeply in love with Him?

LOVING OTHERS WITHOUT FAVORITISM (James 1:26-27)

- God loves us all. And He calls us to love the rich, the poor, those different from us, our friends, our family, and our enemies. Who is easy for you to love? Who is difficult for you to love? How can you nourish your love for others?

5. PRESENTING OURSELVES TO GOD (ROMANS 12:1; EPHESIANS 5:25-27)

SUBMISSION TO HIS AUTHORITY AND POWER

- Strong-willed action can be an act of rebellion toward God, or an act of submission to His authority and power. The choice is in the heart. Ask what you need to place on the altar in submission to Him.

WORSHIP AND STEWARDSHIP GIVING

- The art of giving, both back to God and to others, is something we learn from God because His generosity is our greatest example. When we start to understand His motivations for being extravagant, we suddenly find ourselves caught up in wanting to be an expression of that abundance toward people around us. Giving becomes an act of worship that is in participation with God. Maybe it would help to reflect on what you give to God and what you withhold from Him.

LORD'S SUPPER

- When we participate in the symbolic act of worship called the Lord's Supper, or Communion, we embrace Jesus' sacrifice for our sin, and we experience fellowship with Him and with others. Participate in the Lord's Supper with a humble and reflective heart.

FOOT WASHING

- In the world of Jesus, foot washing was common. It was usually done by those of low social rank — by servants and slaves. Jesus, acting as our servant, washed His followers' feet. This practice may seem too strange for you today. Consider how you could "wash the feet of the poor" in some creative way.

FASTING, SACRIFICE, AND SIMPLICITY . . . DISCIPLINE OF PURITY OF BODY AND SPIRIT

- Fast from something for some designated period of time — such as food, sex, the media, e-mail, the Internet, entertainment, etc. Where is God in this experience?

SINGING

- Delight God by singing to Him aloud, alone, and with time to reflect on the words. Or play an instrument for Him as your audience of one.

6. BUILDING GOD'S KINGDOM WITH HIM (ROMANS 12:1-21)

COMMUNITY LIVING

When we love people and care for each other, we are following the ways of Jesus. Explore ways to share your life and your things with those around you.

- What words of encouragement or affirmation could you share, and with whom?
- With whom could you spend some extra time doing something together or just hanging out?
- What resources or things could you offer to another to use or to have? Who?
- How could you open your home to someone in a way that is uniquely you?
- What kind of meals could you cook with others and then share together?
- How can you move closer to the people you want to "do life with"?

WALKING WITH TRUSTED OTHERS
(JAMES 5:16; ROMANS 15:1-2; 1 CORINTHIANS 12–13)

Explore ways to receive protection and community love from others. We can often do too much alone, devoid of a loving community. Yes, it does feel safer to live as an individual and not have to share your mess with others, or walk into someone else's mess with them. But God intended for us to live as a body. In this we are trusting God to use others in our lives when we:

- Find a prayer companion
- Find a mentor
- Find a trusted other with whom we can be vulnerable
- Share our struggles with another
- Ask another for encouragement
- Ask another for perspective
- Allow another to meet one of your needs

ACTS OF KINDNESS

- Simply greeting your neighbor (or anyone else) can open up relationship (see Matthew 5:47).
- Serve your coworkers or classmates.
- Harder. Serve someone who could never repay you. Serve someone who has treated you unkindly, or serve an enemy.
- Later journal how God met you in these experiences as you took little initiatives.

MEALS TOGETHER

- When we eat, we symbolically admit that we are not self-sufficient and that we need a personal Provider. Invite someone to eat a meal with you, and talk about how you both experience the Provider God who loves you.

ACTS OF JUSTICE WITH MERCY

- Stand with, offer mercy and help to, or give a voice to some person or social group who is powerless in their own circumstances. Consider volunteering with an organization that is promoting redemption in a broken place or to people with broken lives, regardless of whether or not it is overtly "Christian." Later, process how God met you in this experience.

RECONCILE ACROSS RACIAL, GENDER, AND ETHNIC DIVIDES.

- Identify some racial, gender, or ethnic groups that your group is in tension with, or who are historical enemies. Commit to pray, build friendships, seek understanding, forgiveness, and mercy across these divides.

SHARING YOUR EXPERIENCE OF GOD AND JESUS WITH OTHERS

- Identify someone around you who might need to know more about God's wonderful story. Look for opportunities to share your story with them, and to connect God's story with their story.

SPIRITUAL WARFARE — RESISTING SATAN AND EVIL

- Over a week's time, pray for the spirit that binds to be bound in your life and in the lives of others. Pray for protection and to be delivered from evil. Embrace the armor of God described in Ephesians 6:10-20. Ask God to help you become comfortable in your armor and to use it well.

BUILDING SOCIETY AND CARING FOR NATURE

- God has given us the privilege to build society and to be caretakers of nature. Participate in some activity that will build society and care for the environment, acting locally and globally.

EXPANDING THE KINGDOM OF GOD

- How are you expanding the kingdom of God across the nations? Can you pray in faith, "Your kingdom come, your will be done on earth as it is in heaven?"

You may want to use the following chart to plan your journey.

1. Underline or circle a few of the "entry points" (second column) that interest you most (the ones you checked above).

2. If you were to intentionally behold God using that method for a week or two, how would you begin? Jot some practical ideas and goals in the third column.

MAIN ROADWAYS	ENTRY POINTS	PLAN
EXAMPLE	Viewing Nature	For the next week, I would like to take a walk in our nearby park several days after work. I'll ask God to speak to me through those surroundings as I enjoy different aspects of natural beauty. Maybe meditate on Genesis 1 and imagine God creating each aspect of the world and universe.
BEHOLDING GOD WHO IS EVERYWHERE	Viewing Nature Reflections on Visual Arts, Spiritual Sexuality	
LISTENING TO GOD WHO SPEAKS	Reading Scripture Reflective Questions Memorize / Meditate Being Taught Silence and Solitude Music, Extended Prayer Time	
TALKING WITH GOD WHO LISTENS	Prayer Journaling Creating Reflective Healing	
HONESTLY EXAMINING OUR HEARTS BEFORE HIM	Confessing and Repenting Affections and Desires Facing Deep Emotions Eternal Realities Loving God Loving Others	

MAIN ROADWAYS	ENTRY POINTS	PLAN

PRESENTING OURSELVES TO GOD	Submission to Him
	Worship and Stewardship
	   Giving
	Lord's Supper
	Foot Washing
	Fasting, Sacrifice, and
	   Simplicity
	Singing	

BUILDING GOD'S KINGDOM WITH HIM	Community Living
	Walking with Trusted
	   Others
	Acts of Kindness
	Meals Together
	Acts of Justice with
	   Mercy
	Reconciling Across Racial
	   and Economic Barriers
	Sharing Christ
	Spiritual Warfare
	Building Society and
	   Caring for Nature
	Expanding the Kingdom
	   of God	

PERSONAL PROCESSING

Select one way to behold God and actually experience it this week — daily, if possible. In the next months, enjoy beholding God using other methods. Consider trying something from each roadway. Where do you tend to hang out? Consider experimenting with other areas. But don't feel compelled to do all of them! This is a lifetime journey of beholding God and being transformed into His image.

SMALL GROUP PROCESSING

Be prepared to share your "beholding" experiences with your group. Also discuss with your group members how you might behold God together.

CELEBRATING YOUR GROUP

Somewhere deep down, we know that if we are to survive we must come together and rediscover ways to connect with each other, and with the earth that supports our collective life. We are social beings who need one another not just for physical survival but also for spiritual sustenance as we journey together. So our individuality only makes sense in the context of community, where we are free to become ourselves.

— JONATHAN S. CAMPBELL WITH JENNIFER CAMPBELL, *THE WAY OF JESUS*

As you and your group finish this study, it's a good time to celebrate together. Your relationships have deepened through these past weeks. You've learned much from each other — truths, joys, pains. So we encourage you to plan a celebration. Take some time to "Reflect Back," "Envision Forward," and "Pause to Affirm and Pray."

REFLECT BACK

Share how you've benefited from studying God's Word with this group of fellow spiritual journeyers.

How has your walk with God been affected?

How has your daily lifestyle changed?

What emotions surface as you reflect on your times together?

ENVISION FORWARD

What are your spiritual needs as you consider the next phase of your journey?

In what environment might these needs be met?

What continuing relationships will you have with the people in this group (casual friendship to in-depth involvement)?

Are there other people you know who could benefit from studying this series?

Would one or more people from this group facilitate a new group? Is God leading anyone to be a part of a new group?

PAUSE TO AFFIRM

Do you want to express a thank you or affirmation to anyone in the group who has influenced your life? Take time to do that.

PAUSE TO PRAY

Spend time together praying. Thank God for this part of your journey. Praise Him for who He is. Linger longer together.

WHY MEMORIZE SCRIPTURE?

You won't find the word *memorize* in the Bible. But the concept is there both in command and in example ("treasure . . . store up . . . hide" God's words in our hearts). We are encouraged to "study . . . reflect on . . . delight in . . . not forget" God's words (Psalm 119:9-16, NLT; 37:31)

- "lay hold of . . . pay attention . . . listen closely . . . keep [God's words] within your heart" (Proverbs 4:4,20-22).
- "bind them [my commands] around your neck . . . write them on the tablet of your heart" (Proverbs 3:3).
- "always treasure my commands. . . . Guard my instructions as you guard your own eyes. Tie them on your fingers as a reminder. . . . Write them on the tablet of your heart" (Proverbs 7:1-3, NLT, NIV).
- "it is good to keep these sayings in your heart" (Proverbs 22:18, NLT).
- "meditate on [God's words] day and night" (Joshua 1:8).

These same verses also explain the reasons for and benefits of memorizing Scripture:

- "that I might not sin against you . . . [my] feet do not slip" (Psalm 119:9-16; 37:31).
- "they bring life . . . and healing to their whole body" (Proverbs 4:22, NLT).
- "find favor with both God and people . . . earn a good reputation" (Proverbs 3:3-4, NLT).
- "you will trust in the LORD" (Proverbs 22:18-19, NLT).
- "you will be sure to obey everything written in it. Only then will you prosper and succeed" (Joshua 1:8, NLT).
- so that you'll "have all of them ready on your lips" (Proverbs 22:18).
- "your words . . . were my joy and my heart's delight" (Jeremiah 15:16).

Perhaps even more compelling than these reasons is seeing how powerfully God can use a person who has taken the time and effort to consistently memorize Scripture. When Jesus faced Satan (see Matthew 4:1-11), He drew from the many verses of Scripture that He had memorized in His youth to pinpoint Satan's deception and resist temptation. Where would we be if Jesus had not memorized Scripture? When Peter addressed the huge crowd on the day of Pentecost, he was given no time to consult his concordance and prepare a message! Because he had made Scripture memory a priority in his life, he could quote from three different Old Testament passages that helped bring 3,000 people to the Lord!

If you long to equip yourself to counteract Satan, resist sin, trust and obey God, listen to God's voice, and minister to others, there is no better investment of your time than memorizing Scripture.

A good place to begin is by revisiting the verses you memorized here in this study. Carry the verses around. Put them on your PDA. Put them on your computer. Review them out loud. Often. Write them out until you can say them accurately. Meditate on them. Pray over them. Tell a friend what they mean to you. Put yourself to sleep at night thinking about them. And look forward to listening to God speak to you!

I am amazed at the countless times God pulled from my mind a memorized verse that has been exactly the right thing at the right time! At times it was a comfort, at times guidance. A push ahead or a pull to stop. A reminder of His promise, a prompting for wisdom. A word for counseling another, an insight for those seeking our Lord.

— DENNIS STOKES

SCRIPTURE MEMORY VERSES

MEANING OF SEXUALITY

GENESIS 2:24-25

For this reason a man will leave his father and mother and be united to his wife, and they will become one flesh. The man and his wife were both naked, and they felt no shame.

GODLY JEALOUSY

HOSEA 2:19-20

I will betroth you to me forever; I will betroth you in righteousness and justice, in love and compassion. I will betroth you in faithfulness, and you will acknowledge the Lord.

MALE AND FEMALE

GENESIS 1:27

So God created man in his own image, in the image of God he created him; male and female he created them.

HUSBANDS AND WIVES, MEN AND WOMEN
1 PETER 3:4,7

You [women] should clothe yourselves instead with the beauty that comes from within, the unfading beauty of a gentle and quiet spirit, which is so precious to God. . . .

In the same way, you husbands must give honor to your wives. Treat your wife with understanding as you live together. She may be weaker than you are, but she is your equal partner in God's gift of new life. Treat her as you should so your prayers will not be hindered. (NLT)

PROTECTING SEXUALITY

2 TIMOTHY 2:22

Run from anything that stimulates youthful lusts. Instead, pursue righteous living, faithfulness, love, and peace. Enjoy the companionship of those who call on the Lord with pure hearts. (NLT)

LIVING SEXUALITY WELL

1 TIMOTHY 5:1-2

Treat younger men as brothers, older women as mothers, and younger women as sisters, with absolute purity.

EMOTIONAL HEALTH

PROVERBS 4:23

Above all else, guard your heart, for it is the wellspring of life.

EMOTIONAL HEALING

PSALM 147:3

He heals the brokenhearted and bandages their wounds. (NLT)

BEHOLDING GOD

2 CORINTHIANS 3:18

And we, who with unveiled faces all reflect the Lord's glory, are being transformed into his likeness with ever-increasing glory, which comes from the Lord, who is the Spirit.

SERIES OVERVIEW

CONNECT is designed to help you discover and embrace the truth Jesus spoke of in a holistic way. We long to see you enjoying life as a member of God's kingdom and family, deeply experiencing His presence, knowing His truth, resting in His love, and confident in His hope. These studies are designed to be used in small groups where people can encourage, trust, and support each other on their spiritual journeys.

CONNECT is arranged as a series of Bible studies. These studies will present foundational biblical principles for primary relationships in life. Jesus summed up what life is all about when He said, "'Love the Lord your God with all your heart and with all your soul and with all your mind.' This is the first and greatest commandment. And the second is like it: 'Love your neighbor as yourself'" (Matthew 22:37-39). Growing in your love for God, for others, and for yourself while managing your personal life in ways that honor Him — now that is a real spiritual journey!

ABOUT THE AUTHORS

RALPH ENNIS is the Director of Intercultural Training and Development for The Navigators. Ralph and his wife, Jennifer, have ministered with The Navigators since 1975 in a variety of areas, including at Norfolk military bases, Princeton University, Richmond Community, Glen Eyrie Leadership Development Institute, and with The CoMission in Moscow, Russia. Ralph has a Master's degree in Intercultural Relations. Some of his publications include *Searching the Ordinary for Meaning; Breakthru: Discover Your Spiritual Gifts and Primary Roles; Successfit: Decision Making Preferences; An Introduction to the Russian Soul;* and *The Issue of Shame in Reaching People for Christ.*

Ralph and Jennifer currently live in Raleigh, North Carolina. They have four married children and nine grandchildren.

JUDY GOMOLL is Director of School Agreements as a National Training Team Associate. Before joining The Navigators, Judy was an educator with a specialty in curriculum development. Judy and her husband, George, served with The Navigators as missionaries in Uganda and Kenya for fifteen years, where they helped pioneer ministries in communities, churches, and at Makerere University. Judy led in leader training and designing of contextualized discipleship materials and methods.

In her current role with the National Training Team, Judy is assisting in the research, development, and field testing of spiritual transformation training tools and resources. She also directs our partnerships agreements with seminaries and graduate schools.

Judy has an MA in Curriculum and Instruction, and an MA in Organizational Leadership. She and George live in Parker, Colorado.

DENNIS STOKES is Director of National Training and Staff Development. Dennis has been serving with The Navigators since 1980, ministering with the Collegiate Mission, as well as being a collegiate trainer and training consultant. Dennis has designed, developed, and led seven Navigator summer training programs, and was the Training Coordinator for The CoMission project. Dennis has done gospel ministry in Lebanon, Russia, Ukraine, Mexico, Canada, England, Cyprus, Egypt, Jordan, Syria, and Israel. He is ordained and speaks at training events, conferences, and in church pulpits both in the U.S. and overseas. In his role as the National Training Director for the U.S. Navigators, Dennis leads in strategic planning, leading, and implementing all national initiatives for staff training and development.

Dennis and his wife, Ellen, live in Boulder, Colorado, and have three children, Christopher, Cheryl, and Amy.

CHRISTINE WEDDLE is Associate Director of National Training and Staff Development and has been on staff with The Navigators since 1997. She first connected with The Navigators when she joined the CoMission Training Team. In this role she assisted in the planning and organization of staff training events in the U.S., Russia, and the Ukraine.

Since moving to Colorado Springs in 1998, she has directed numerous national training and staff development events. She specializes in developing adult learning environments and visual resources.

REBECCA GOLDSTONE is a National Training Team consultant for The Navigators. Before joining The Navigators, Rebecca was a consulting partner with The Navigators in training and developing The CoMission project staff and leaders from the former Soviet countries. After leaving The CoMission Rebecca pioneered and developed a crosscultural urban ministry in Santa Ana, California. She is a training consultant, life coach, and serves on the faculty of Hope International University. Her role on the National Training Team consists of creating and editing resources related to spiritual transformation and strategic tools to equip leaders ministering to the millennial generation.

Rebecca and her husband, Marc, live in Irvine, California. They have two children, Ryan and Joshua.

Connect Even More!

The CONNECT series is designed to help you discover and embrace the truth Jesus spoke of in a holistic way. By using the series in a small group, you will find encouragement, trust, and support from others as you travel together on this spiritual journey.

God: Connecting with His Outrageous Love

Ralph Ennis, Judy Gomoll, Dennis Stokes, Christine Weddle
978-1-60006-258-2
1-60006-258-X

This study presents a foundational biblical principle for primary relationships in life: receiving God's love and loving Him in response.

Identity: Becoming Who God Says I Am

Ralph Ennis, Judy Gomoll, Dennis Stokes, Christine Weddle
978-1-60006-259-9
1-60006-259-8

Discover who God says you are and learn to live out your true identity by loving God, others, and yourself.

Relationships: Bringing Jesus into My World

Ralph Ennis, Judy Gomoll, Rebecca Goldstone, Dennis Stokes, Christine Weddle
9-781-60006-261-2
1-60006-261-X

Receiving God's love and in turn loving others is God's plan for us. But loving others as ourselves is not always easy. Learn how to reach out in love to family, friends, and others who may be more difficult to love.

Life: Thriving in a Complex World

Ralph Ennis, Judy Gomoll, Rebecca Goldstone, Dennis Stokes, Christine Weddle
978-1-60006-260-5
1-60006-260-1

Explore important areas—time, money, decisions, commitment—that play a role in living life well with Jesus.

To order copies, call NavPress at 1-800-366-7788, or log on to www.navpress.com.

NAVPRESS

BE TRANSF**ORM**ED